INDIA'S HOOD UNVEILED

(1910)

SOUTH INDIA MYSTERIES

&

ASTRAL AND SPIRIT SIGHT

Contents: Hindu Hypnograph; Ancient Hindu Method for Hindu Clairvoyance; Levitation; Method of Suspended Animation; Spirit Sight at Will.

L. W. de Laurence

ISBN 1-56459-926-4

INDIA'S HOOD UNVEILED

SOUTH INDIA MYSTERIES

𝔅𝔬𝔬𝔨 𝔒𝔫𝔢

ASTRAL AND SPIRIT SIGHT

HINDU HYPNOGRAPH ANCIENT HINDU METHOD OR HIND
CLAIRVOYANCE HINDU LEVITATION (RAISING THE
HUMAN BODY IN THE AIR). HINDU METHOD OF
BURIAL ALIVE, (SUSPENDED ANIMATION)
SPIRIT SIGHT AT WILL

IN THREE PARTS

BY A NATIVE HINDU OF SOUTH INDIA

Prepared for publication under the editorship of

DR. L. W. de LAURENCE

*"Author of The Great Book of Magical Art, Hindu Magic,
and East Indian Occultism," "The Mystic Text Book
of the Hindu Occult Chamber," "The
Famous Book of Death," etc, etc.*

Published exclusively in the United States by

THE de LAURENCE COMPANY
Chicago, Ill., U. S. A 1910

Preface to Book One.

If you are wise and want good results you will keep these teachings to yourself.

The Sages of yore, our forefathers, are the discoverers of this wonderful and mighty power, which is even now practiced by many a yogi and fakir, and whose ability and display of skill have conveyed startling proofs which have established a standing glory for this Science. What that was bequeathed to us, in sacred trust, should not be neglected and allowed to die almost a natural death. This is no work of the dreamy theorists of the present day, but of men who have spent years of study and experiment, and those who have led a life far different from that of ordinary men. The fruit of their labour is now laid before you.

Indians, whose religious rituals and ceremonies are imbued and pregnant with the elementary as well as advanced principles of Occultism, which lead to the higher phases—Yoga, Clairvoyance, Clairaudience, etc.—have more facilities to learn this science than others.

Now, this subject which is at once novel and interesting, though the truths conveyed are aged as the world and so simple as to appear useless, at one time, did command the attention of wiser heads than ours.

A mastery of this science means a thorough knowledge of the Philosophy of Human nature and the Development of your Soul.

(5)

It is for you to decide whether you will direct or be directed, whether you will command or be commanded, whether you will rise or fall.

Self-esteem, stubbornness, and an arrogant, haughty disposition do not go to make up, of you, a commander, but you should be made of a different sort of sterner stuff, which will raise you to praise, power and glory. The Omnipotent and All Benevolent Creator has not created masters and servants in this world, and it is you and you alone that go to make yourself. If you put forth proper effort to cultivate and put into motion, the power that is latent and inborn in you, the door to success is within your reach; and it is for you to open it.

WHAT HYPNOTISM IS!

What we present to you in this book is a simple entrance into the realm of practice and of the wonders and possibilities of Hypnotism. There seems to be a widespread delusion that Hypnotism is some special and august power through which the possessor dominates the minds and will-powers of those with whom he comes in contact and renders them mere automatons. Hypnotism is the induction of a state which has no physiological difference from that produced by natural sleep, as the same faculties that are dormant and active in the natural sleep, are also dormant and active in the Hypnotic sleep. It is one of the most innocent agents known to modern science. Probably no other science means so much to the individual and surely, no other may be so quickly and so easily mastered. A knowledge of it awakens a man to his latent possibilities and teaches him to respect himself and to appreciate his proper relation to his fellow-men. It makes him self-centered and confident; it begets in him an irresistible momentum and makes him master of his own thought and action. It is a valuable Therapeutic agent in all diseases of the nervous system, and since all diseases have their nervous aspect, it is of universal use in the relief of the suffering.

We are convinced that the time is fast approaching when physicians will place as much confidence in Hypnotism as in Medicine, if not more.

No doubt all admit the great and wonderful possibilities of this science and its value as a Therapeutic agent; but no one has hitherto unravelled the reasons for the wonderful phenomena evidenced during the practice of Hypnotism and never will be able until man is able to grasp more of the working of the human brain than all physiologists and psychologists have hitherto done. There is a vast field for the intending explorers as some of the advanced metaphysicians of the day have even thrown out the stupendous theory that "death is simply a habit."

The writers on the subjects usually conclude by telling their readers of the wonderful possibilities open to any one who can acquire this power and learn how to use it. They, however, say little or nothing of how this force may be acquired, that is, beyond stating their theories. They deliver discourse—but do not instruct. They are preachers—not teachers. They dwell upon theories—neglect facts.

We leave the land of theory and enter into the realm of practice, and will endeavor to instruct you along the lines of development and the use of this mighty force that you may reproduce the results already obtained by others and perhaps may become investigators and leaders in the work of blazing the way through the wood of superstition and mystery in which the subject has been so long shrouded.

If you grasp the elementary principles of Hypnotism, you will be the master of the laws through which the human mind is moulded and swayed and of that intangible and subtle power which controls where even daggers fail.

Patience and perseverance is the price of success. It matters not how unimportant our instructions may seem to you, or how simple they may appear; make up your mind to follow them in every detail; do not pass judgment upon a thing until you have given it a fair trial; remember the greatest things in life are often the simplest things. It may seem to you that our instructions are so simple to produce the astounding results which we claim for them, but if you will only give them a thorough trial you will be more enthusiastic in their praises than we.

Study this book carefully and you will feel astounded at your success and the number of people you are able to influence and hypnotize. The salient and all important advice we give you is *"Learn each lesson before taking up the next."* Unless you succeed in the first and until you succeed in that, you should not take up the next lesson. If you proceed contrary to our directions, we are not responsible for your success. Remember, the instructions now laid before you are the foundation over which you will have to build the structure of success. It is the key, and without it the doors of Occultism will not be opened to you. Master it well and your complete success is certain.

India's
Hood Unveiled

𝕭𝖔𝖔𝖐 𝕺𝖓𝖊

CHAPTER I.

LESSON 1.

PERSONAL MAGNETISM.

Personal Magnetism is that quality in man which attracts interest, confidence, friendship and love of man kind. This is the secret of success.

To be successful in this branch of science, the following should be strictly adhered to:

1. THE ART OF INTELLIGENT LISTENING AND CONVERSING.—In conversation observe the following rules. Never interrupt a person while speaking; appear to pay attention and to be interested in the conversation, but do not let his thoughts produce any real impression upon you. Avoid arguments on any and all subjects, for every one has got his own opinions. Do not attract attention by either your loud talk or laughter, or show your ego-

tism by trying to absorb in conversation. Avoid whispering or conversing in a language that all the parties may not be acquainted with. If you are gifted with wit, do not make a display of it. Do not use slangwords and never indulge in idle or ill natured gossip. Do not boast of your achievements. Never make fun of the peculiarities or idosyncracies of people with whom you come in contact.

Always be simple, neat and clean. Keep your body clean and void of any bad odour, and let your clothes be brushed and neat.

2. A PLEASANT AND CHEERFUL MANNER.—Be always polite, for politeness is the oil that lubricates society. Avoid arrogance and sycophancy. Be plain and unassuming. Study the characteristics of each and every man whom you wish to influence. Never get excited in conversation. Always be obliging and ready to assist others out of misfortunes and dilemmas. Be as agreeable to your social inferiors as to your equals and superiors.

3. PHYSICAL AND MORAL FEARLESSNESS.—If you are quick tempered and apt to give way to a fear of misfortune or worry, you should pay particular attention to the lessons given in the Advanced Course under "Will Power."

4. EARNESTNESS IN TALKING.—Cultivate a frank and open manner. Always be earnest when you talk. It not only holds the attention of the people to whom you are talking, but it is also a valuable aid to you.

5. A MANLY HAND SHAKE.—When you first meet a person whom you wish to influence, shake hands with him, if it is convenient, in the following manner: Grasp the hand firmly but not so hard as to cause pain; take hold of as much of the hand, never take hold of the fingers. Take the hand quickly so that the person cannot shut his fingers down and prevent you from grasping the full hand. Then shake his hand up and down once only; and when you get to the down shake, hold the hand a few seconds and as you draw your hand away let your

fingers pass slowly over the first finger. In shaking hands it is well to bring your body slightly forward towards the individual and look at the root of his nose without winking or blinking and think in your mind firmly what you wish him to do.

6. AN AGREEABLE TONE OF VOICE.—This forms one of the important features in the acquisition of Personal Magnetism. Cultivate an agreeable tone of voice, avoiding a mumbling utterance on the one hand and a loud, boisterous tone on the other. An excellent rule is to pitch the voice to the tone of the party with whom you are conversing, providing always that you do not shout, in order to keep pace with the other person. If the other man shouts, keep your own voice even and subdued and he will soon drop to your pitch.

7. PHYSICAL CONTROL.—Every acton in man is loss of energy or magnetism. Therefore an would-be psychologist must first learn not to make any movement without reason. It is necessary that you must accustom yourself to sit still for 5 to 10 minutes at a time without the least movement of any organ of the body. Of course, the moving of the eyelids is excepted, as you cannot control it in this initial stage. You must not allow your thoughts to roam anywhere else but on the act that you wish to keep quiet. This will take some time and you will find it difficult in the beginning to follow. Stick to it and in a short time you will see what you can do. The movements of your body must be done slowly and with ease, as any sudden jerk would waste the magnetism in you. It is on this principle that the followers of Yoga are asked to resume certain postures which would not allow any movement at all.

8. MAGNETIC EYE.—The eye is the all-potent factor in influencing people. It not only seems to hold the attention of the person to whom you are talking, but it is also a power in impressing your will upon another. The eye of the man who has mastered the laws of mental control is a powerful weapon. You have heard of the power of the human eye over wild beasts and savages.

We give you the following exercises which will aid you in acquiring that Magnetic gaze, which is an important acquisition for the student of personal influence. This is a most interesting study, and you will have the pleasure of seeing the increase of the power of your eye manifested by the people, who will become restless and uneasy beneath your gaze and will even manifest fear if you concentrate your gaze upon them for a few seconds. When once you have mastered you will not part with your gift even for hundred times the amount you have paid for the course.

LESSON 1.

THE MIRROR EXERCISE.—Place a small mirror on a table before you, or stand before a large mirror with your face about 15 inches from the mirror. Make a little dot with ink on the root of your nose directly between the eyes. Fix your eyes steadily upon the black spot (in the mirror) and gaze at it firmly without winking. When you feel impelled to wink simply raise the lids a little instead and you will have perfect relief. Practice this until you can gaze at the mirror without winking for 15 minutes together at a time.

LESSON 2.

THE CARDBOARD EXERCISE.—Take a piece of white cardboard about 6 inches square, upon which draw a circle about the size of a silver 4-anna piece and fill the circle with black ink. Stand erect, facing the wall at a distance of 3 feet. Now place your cardboard in tronf of you, with the spot directly in front of your eyes. Fix your gaze upon the spot and then move your head around in a circle, keeping your gaze fixed upon the spot. As this exercise causes the eyes to roll around in keeping the gaze steady, the nerves and muscles receive considerable exercise. Vary the exercise by circling the head in different directions. Use this exercise mildly at first and avoid tiring the eyes. Continue this until you are able to gaze for 15 minutes together without winking.

LESSON 3.

CIRCULAR INFLUENCE.—Stand with your back against the wall and facing towards the opposite wall, shift your gaze rapidly from one point of the wall to another—right, left, up, down, zig-zag, circle, etc. Period of practice as above.

It is advisable for the student to practice the above exercises each morning upon rising. If your eyes tire by reason of the exercises bathe them in cold water and you will experience a decided relief. You will find that after a few days' practice, and then you will have little trouble of this kind.

9. BREATHING.—As breath forms one of the chief factors in storing magnetism and is a helper of the law of nature, the following exercise must be practiced:

LESSON 4.

Every morning immediately on rising go to the open window of a room which has free ventilation. Fold your arms across the chest and draw the upper arms close to the side. Stand erect; expel all the air out of your lungs. After a short time relax your arms and hang them at the sides. Inhale deeply through the nostrils as much air as the lungs will hold. The action must commence from the abdomen and then distend the chest. The inhaled air must be held within for 15 seconds and then exhale slowly through the mouth. Practice this not less than 5 times a day. In the beginning you may feel a little dizzy and this will wear off in time.

10. VITALITY.—To add and store up vitality and to make your physique appear attractive, think and practice the following:

(1) At meal times make it a point to masticate every morsel as thoroughly as possible, and think and picture

within yourself that you are extracting a good deal of magnetism from the food.

(2) When practising the breathing implant the idea in your mind that you are absorbing within you Nature's magnetism in abundance.

(3) While taking bath every morning concentrate your idea that you are drawing Healthy Magnetism from the water you bathe in to vivify your system and to make your physique attractive and beautiful.

11. CONCENTRATION.—As concentration is an essential requisite for a student of Personal Magnetism the following simple exercise will be of immense use:

LESSON 5.

Sit in a chair; assume an easy posture; place your hands on your knees, palms upwards. Count till 10 and then begin to flex the fingers of one hand very slowly one by one at a time. Look and think intently of the action till the fingers are closed. Do the same with the other hand also. Again count till ten and then commence to open the fingers of both the hands one by one. Do this exercise for several minutes.

History teaches us that great men like Napoleon and Bismarck had this power of Personal Magnetism in them and used it either consciously or unconsciously in the achievement of every purpose. It is only after mastering Telepathy and Will Power you can be called an expert. The power acquired by the practice of the above few exercises can be put into practical use. If you wish to have a favor of a person, advance boldly to him, intently looking on him (mind, not rudely) with a firm belief and idea that he will accede to your request. Make a short account of your purpose; during the narration when you reach the climax make him look at you by some means or other and throw more force in your words and press him for an answer before he turns away from you. Though you have not been granted your request point blank, it is sure you have influenced him and it will do you some good. When others approach you, think what you would do if you are kept in the position of the suppliant and give him a patient hearing and not in any way be impressed by his talk or argument and do not of all give him a decided answer, but think over the matter after he has left you and then decide once for all. For an advanced student of Personal Magnetism the portals of society are open and he will be the *beau* of the assembly and the rotating wheel of any gathering. Even unconsciously on the part of the student himself, the party assembled will feel an irresistible idea of turning to him for each and every thing and admire him. In short, Personal Magnetism rules the World.

CHAPTER II.

HYPNOTISM.

LESSON 6.

Now you have acquired the power of influencing people in a small way, and it is only a question of time for you to become a successful Hypnotist. You should bear in mind all successful operators and noted hypnotists came to be such only by long practical experience.

First of all you should thoroughly understand what our instructions are and then proceed to work. The instructions should be at your fingers' ends; you should not hesitate what to do next. Generally some of our students read the instructions once or twice and succeed pretty well in hypnotising the first ones. When you have once succeeded you will have a confidence in your ability and it will create a power in you by developing your latent faculties; then hypnotising and influencing people will be a matter of routine with you.

If you do not succeed with the first five or ten you try, do not give up; but keep trying. Try 20 or 30 different persons or more if necessary and just as sure as night follows day you will come across some one whom you can hypnotise. In selecting subjects it would be better if people between the ages of 14 and 30 are first tried. Never try with children under five years. We do not think that the salient advice to try many persons will ever have to be followed by you, as we are sure and know for certain that failure is impossible with us.

(16)

Unlike other Institutes, we deal in the practical side of the question and are not dreamy theorists. No doubt there are one or two institutes in the world which do practical teaching, but they give you an elementary knowledge of the principles of this Science and make you fit to be stage performers, and the higher and nobler part of the branch is entirely left unopened by them.

Further, they first of all introduce you to the main branch—Hypnotism proper—wherein fortunately you may chance to succeed in your first trials and you are made to misjudge your power. When you publicly proceed to give any demonstration, etc., you are beset with difficulties and you find to your chagrin and shame that you are not able to do anything. Unlike them we go step by step and inculcate a power in you (having well understood by long experience the main factors which make one a successful hypnotist). And it is why that we did not introduce you at first to this all important branch. We first trained in you a powerful eye and have made people quail before your gaze. Now you have a royal road laid open before you and you are welcome to enter it and have no stumbling blocks to encounter with.

We do not say, "Be confident, you will succeed," as we know pretty well that you have gained confidence ere long by the testimony of your own abilities.

LESSON 7.

You have now acquired a power in Personal Magnetism and have cultivated the Magnetic gaze. For the purpose of developing this, as well as Hypnotic Influence, we have set up some simple tests. When you succeed in these tests, your success in these Sciences is assured, and you grasp the elementary principles of Hypnotism proper as you go through the whole Course and you will unconsciously develop in yourself the power of hypnotising people.

LESSON 8.

If you wish to ascertain whether one is susceptible to hypnotism, ask him to stand up with his feet together, head up, and his hands at his sides. Tell him to close his eyes and relax his muscles completely. To test whether the subject has relaxed his muscles or not, lightly pull him back and if he falls you may be sure that he has relaxed. Stand behind him and place your hands upon his shoulders for a few seconds—say 30. Fix your gaze at the base of the brain or pit of the neck, and then move down your hands slowly over his backbone. Do this for one minute with a strong intention of drawing him towards you. Now place the tips of your fingers very lightly upon the shoulder blades and very slowly make a dozen downward movements (passes) with your hands. When you do so, suggest in a slow, positive tone, "When — I — withdraw — my — hand — from — you; you — will — fall — backward; you — cannot — resist — falling; you — will — fall — backward."

Then slowly withdraw your hands fro mhis back, in such a way that the person cannot perceive the movements of your hands; and the person will surely fall backward; whilst falling, take care to catch hold of him to prevent him from falling and receiving any hurt. If the person does not fall backward, try him once more and with a little experience in this you will soon acquire a knack in influencing a good number of people. Thus a perfectly wide-awake person, if he is susceptible or sensitive, will be easily affected.

This test is given you simply not to throw any obstacles in your way.

LESSON 9.

How to Make One Spellbound by Your Gaze.— Do not take up this test until you have succeeded in the previous one.

Naturally you may feel a desire to test the power of

your Magnetic eye and this test will prove it to you.

Persuade any of your friends to stand before and look at your eyes for a few seconds. Then suggest mentally, "You will not be able to withstand my gaze; you will quail before me." You should look at the root of his nose (midway between the eyes). On no consideration should you remove your eyes from him even for a single moment. You should clearly instruct him not to look away from you. After one or two minutes he will become uneasy, his mind will be confused and he will implicitly obey you. You should take a great precaution in asking him to do anything that may be against his established principles.

LESSON 10.

FASCINATION.—Do not try this test until you have succeeded in the previous one. For this select some one with whom you have been successful in the above two. Ask him to stand before you and place his hands, palms down, fair and square on the top of yours, your palms being above. Think determinedly that his hands have become fastened to yours so that he cannot take his hands, try he ever so hard. Do not tell him anything until you are ready to suggest in a firm tone: "You— will — find — your — hands — are — sticking — together — tight — tighter — tighter — tight — and — you—cannot—pull—them—away."

During the operation you should look straight in the eyes. The subject also should be impressed not to look away and if he attempts to do so, you should command him to look into your eyes.

You should repeat the suggestion often and often, as suggestions gain strength by repetition. When you find that he is getting uneasy, say in a positive tone, not very fast, "Now — you — will — find — your — hands — sticking—tightly," and keep getting more positive and throw in more energy until you finally suggest that he cannot take his hands apart.

How to Remove the Influence.—When the subject tries to pull his hands apart, and is not able to do so, you should suggest to him very positively, "All—right—wake up—wide awake—all right." You should continue repeating until the influence is completely removed, which in almost all cases will be sudden.

LESSON 11.

How to Make One Go Down Upon His Knees.— Ask some one with whom you have been successful in the previous tests to stand before you. Take hold of his right hand and place it on top of your left hand. Look at the root of his nose intently, willing that he will kneel down. Make a number of downward passes with your hand in front of his body down to his knees. And then suggest, "You — are — going — down — down — on —your—knees; you are kneeling—kneeling—kneel— kneel—kneel—down." And he will surely kneel. To remove the influence do as instructed in Test No. 3.

LESSON 12.

How to Make One Unable to Kneel Down.—Remember, you should not under any circumstances undertake this unless you have mastered the previous ones.

Instruct your subject to place his full weight upon his knees, while you take hold of one of his hands. Keep your gaze directly at the root of his nose. Mind, this is an important point in influencing people. Tell him to look straight in your eyes and to think that he cannot kneel down.

You should kneel before the subject and give 5 or 6 passes, commencing 6 inches above the knee and continuing 6 inches down the knee. During the whole time your eye should be at the root of his nose, and when you rise, his eyes should follow yours. When making the passes say in a very positive tone: "Now—you—will— find — your — legs — are — getting — stiff — stiff —

stiffer — stiff; you — cannot — kneel — down." Leave him in that state a few seconds and then say: "All right —wake up," etc., as explained in the previous lesson.

LESSON 13.

How to Make One Unable to Bend His Arm.—Ask your subject to stretch out his arm and close the fingers. As in the previous lesson make his arm stiff. Then take hold of his fist by your left hand and make a few passes with your right hand down inside of arm and at the same time suggest: "Your—arm—is—getting —stiff — stiff — stiffer — stiffer — stiff — very — stiff; and—you—cannot—bend—your—arm; the more you try the more you cannot." After a few seconds remove the influence as before.

LESSON 14

How to Make One Unable to Open His Mouth.—Tell your subject to shut his mouth. As instructed in the preceding lesson tighten his jaws. Look at the root of his nose and let him look at your eyes. Your gaze should not be removed from him even for a moment. Make passes from the lobes of his ears down to the chin with both your hands simultaneously, saying: "Your— jaws — are — getting — tight — tight — tighter — tighter — tight — very — tight; you — cannot — open —your—mouth." After some time remove the influence.

LESSON 15.

How to Keep a Person From Throwing a Ruler Down.—Let your subject take hold of a ruler and tell him to look into your eyes and grasp the ruler as tight as possible. Now look at the root of his nose with a firm, steady gaze for 30 seconds and suggest, after telling him to think that he cannot let go the ruler and that he will find the ruler sticking to his hands when you

count three: "Ready—one—two—three—now—you—
cannot — throw — the — ruler — down; try —the more
—you—try—the more—you—cannot." After a time remove the influence.

LESSON 16.

HOW TO MAKE ONE TO RAISE HIS LEG.—Take the
subject with whom you have been successful in the previous test and make him sit upon a chair and cross one
leg over the other. Give a few passes over the upper-
most leg for a short time, and then make a few drawing
passes as if you were lifting the toe towards you; his
leg will, of its own accord, rise along with the passes.
You should also think firmly that the leg should rise.
The subject will not be able to resist the influence. When
the leg has taken an almost horizontal position say in a
positive tone: "Now—you—cannot—put—down—your
—leg; it—will—stand—in—the—air; you—cannot—put
—it—down." Then remove the influence by lightly pat-
ting over the leg from the foot up to the thigh and say:
"Now — you — can — put — down — your — leg; you
—are—all—right—wake up—wide awake."

LESSON 17.

METHODS OF INDUCING HYPNOTIC SLEEP.—To put one
into hypnotic sleep we give you the best and most tried
and sure methods.

For this select some one with whom you have been
hitherto successful.

Request your subject to seat himself conveniently on
a high-backed chair or lie down on a bed. Take any
bright object, for instance, a golden ring or a silver button (bright), and hold it so much above the eyes that his
eyelids are strained as much as possible in having the
eyes opened. You should now move the object round
and round in a circle, having a diameter of, say, 4 inches.
You should rotate the object until you find a closing of

your subject's eyes. Then lay aside the object. While rotating the object, suggest the following in a low rhythmic tone: "Now—your—eyelids—are—beginning—to—close; your—eyes—are—growing—more—and— more — tired; the lids—quiver—more—and—more; you—feel—tired—all—over; your—eyes—close; now—your—eyelids —are—closed—Sleep—go—sound—asleep." Do this for five minutes.

LESSON 18.

Now place your fingers of the left hand on the crown of the subject's head and the thumb on his forehead; place your thumb of the right hand on the left of his forehead. Move the right thumb slowly from centre of forehead down over the root of nose. Continue this for 5 minutes. While moving the thumb suggest: "Sleepy —sleep—sleepy—sound asleep—sound asleep—sleep— —sleepy—sleep," etc. Your tone should be slow and positive and the pressure of your right thumb should not in any way hurt the subject.

Great care should be taken in giving the suggestions. The art can be cultivated only by long practice.

Stand behind the subject and place the tips of your fingers of both hands on the back part of neck below the head and move them down slowly down to the shoulders so as to cause a little quivering, pleasant sensation. Keep doing this for four minutes. During the whole process suggest sleep formulæ.

LESSON 19.

Stand on the right-hand side in front of the subject, place your left thumb on the root of his nose, and your other fingers on the crown of his head. Let your right hand hang down by your side. Look at the root of his nose and repeat the following sleep formulæ in a positive, firm and rhythmic tone: "Your — eyes — are — tightly—closed; you—cannot—open—them; your—arms

—go—to—sleep; your—hands—are—motionless; your—legs—grow—tired; you—cannot—move; you—cannot—feel—anything; you—are—going—sound asleep—sleep—sleep—sleepy—sleepy — sleep — sound asleep — sound asleep — your—head—feels—duller; your—limbs—are—heavy; your—thoughts—grow—more—and—more—confused; now—you—are—so—sleepy — when — I — count — three — you—will—fall—into—a—deep—sleep. Now —one—two—three—sleep—fast asleep." This should be repeated for five minutes or even longer if necessary.

LESSON 20.

Have your subject seated on a high-back chair and take yourself a seat and have your eye in a level with the subject's. Ask the subject to cross his arms. Then take hold of his right hand by your left and his left by your right; hold them in such a position that your thumbs touch the back of the subject's hands just below the knuckles of the 2nd and 3rd fingers. Ask the subject to look into your eyes and do not allow him to turn the gaze from you on any account. After a minute or two suggest, slowly: "You feel a tingling sensation in your hands; the sensation slowly extends to your whole body; your eyes are growing fatigued; you cannot have them open; your eyes are closing; you are going asleep; sleep, sleep," etc. A few passages from the top of the head down to the knees will be of great use.

At the close of half of an hour from the beginning, if the subject is not asleep, you should discontinue the work. Then take the subject on the next day at the same hour and try for 30 minutes.

Many persons will go to sleep in a very short time. Then the work may be discontinued and the sleep formulæ also omitted to a certain extent. The whole process will occupy only from five to ten minutes except in very difficult cases, which may require the maximum time of thirty minutes.

When you learn these methods turn to page 17 and

study carefully the methods of awakening the subject from sleep. It is only when you have clearly understood them you can undertake to do any experiments.

LESSON 21.

HOW TO PRODUCE SUDDEN HYPNOSIS.—A combination of any two of the above methods will result in bringing the subject to a speedy hypnotic condition. In place of bright objects you may provide yourself with a glass ball to give a mystic appearance. It is quite unnecessary to waste money in the so-called Hypnotic Balls. A common glass ball with a coating of mercury in the inside generally sold in the bazaars will serve the purpose. And if you cannot procure such a one or you are not able to get even a ring or a button you may just as well ask the subject to close his eyes and proceed with your work. If you particularly wish to have one, we can provide you with one at a moderate cost.

To save time, for entertainers who may not find it at their disposal, the above combined methods are useful But many people cannot be hypnotised under such con ditions It is only with experienced operator, that in stantaneously astonishing effects are produced.

LESSON 22.

HOW TO HYPNOTISE A SUBJECT WHILE LYING DOWN.—Tell your patient to lie on his back or right side; hold his right hand with your left, letting your thumb rest in the centre on the back part of the palm of the patient's right hand about midway between the knuckles and the wrist, and let the fingers of your left hand rest in the palm of your subject's right. Now pass your right hand across his forehead over the temples and down to the cheek bone. Make these "passes at contact," with your right hand, for 10 or 15 minutes, and suggest in a positive tone with your gaze firmly implanted at the root of nose: "Sleep—sleepy—sleepy—sleep; you—are—get-

ting—tired; you—feel—drowsy; everything—is—getting
—dark—to—you; you—are—so—sleepy—you—can—not
—hear—any—thing—except—my—voice; and—when—I
—count—ten—you—will — be — sound—asleep. One —
two — three — four — five — six — seven — eight —
nine — ten; sleep — s-o-u-n-d — a-s-l-e-e-p — f-a-s-t
a-s-l-e-e-p." Repeat these suggestions five or six times.
Then we would advise you to place your right hand over
the subject's and as he exhales the breath, lightly press
downward, and when he inhales, release the pressure
and suggest: "You—are—breathing—deeper; you—are
—breathing—deeper; you—are—sound asleep; sleep—
fast asleep."

To make the subject go still deeper, it is better you
commence to breathe very deeply once or twice yourself
and we are quite certain that your subject will also
breathe deeply and in a short time usually drop into deep
hypnosis.

LESSON 23.

How to Hypnotise by Numbers.—Seat your subject
or subjects in a high-backed chain or bench in a comfortable position. Tell your subject to be passive and request
him to look at you. Now begin counting, "1—2—3—4
—5—6—7—8—9," etc., in a slow, rhythmic way, looking at the root of his nose. In the meanwhile instruct
your subject to close his eyes at each "odd" number and
to open at every "even" number. Continue to count very
slowly "a hundred," if necessary; generally by the time
you count a "fifty" your subject will go asleep.

From practical experience we tell you that many subjects will be unable to open their eyes by the time you
count twenty. In such cases continue to count a little
longer. As you do this your subject may raise his eyelids, under the impression that he is opening and closing
his eyes. After a time, you may notice a dropping of
his head in a very drowsy condition. Then it is better

you make some "passes at contact" over the temples, repeating the sleep formulæ as already explained.

LESSON 24.

How to Hypnotise by a Tumbler of Water.—Get your subject seated in a high-backed chair. Procure a tumbler of ice-cold water and dip your fingers in it. Then commence to give passes at contact from the forehead down to the chin and suggest: "Your—eyes—are —closing; your—eyes—are—closing; your—eyes—have —closed; you—cannot—open—them; your—efforts—to —open are useless; sleep—sleep—sleepy—sleep—sound —asleep."

Another method is to make a few passes over the tumbler of water and then to ask the subject to drink it slowly. Assert positively that he will sleep within a short time after he has drunk the water. Give a few passes from the top of the head down to the abdomen and suggest: "Sleep—sleep," etc.

LESSON 25.

How to Hypnotise With a Silver Coin.—Seat your subject in a high-backed chair. Take a bright silver four-anna piece, and request him to hold it between the thumb, fore and middle fingers of his left hand. Then allow his left hand to rest in the hollow of his right and let his hands be about 12 inches from his eyes. Instruct him to keep his eyes steadily fixed on the coin. Allow him to continue this as long as you notice a contraction and dilation of the pupils of his eyes. Then slowly ask him to move his hands a little farther from his eyes. Mostly the eyelids will close involuntarily with a vibratory motion. Now suggest in a positive manner: "Shut up—and—sleep." Allow him some time, say 3 or 4 minutes, and by that time the subject will fall asleep.

Another Method.—Hold the coin in your right hand in a level with the subject's eye—say at a distance of

15 inches. Place your right hand on the wrist of the subject over the radial artery and watch the pulse carefully. In a short time you will see that his heart beats rapidly, his pulse becomes bounding and the eyes dilate. Then suggest: "Your—eyelids—are—growing—heavy; you — feel — the — warm — blood — coursing — through—your—veins; you—cannot—have—your—eyelids—open; shut up; sleep; fast asleep." And at the same time stroke his right hand and suggest: "Your—limbs —are—growing—heavy; your—limbs—are—heavy· sleep—fast—asleep—now."

LESSON 26.

HYPNOSIS BY THE AID OF A WATCH OR CLOCK.—Place a chair with its back against a table. Now ask your subject to sit on the chair. Place a watch or a clock on the table. Take care that you select a room which is free from noise and disturbance. Tell him to attend to the ticking of the watch and let not his attention be diverted by anything else and at the same time to look at the tip of his nose. By the monotonous ticking of the watch and the constant staring at the tip of the nose the senses will attain a sleepy sensation and, consequently, the subject will fall asleep within a very short time. As in the previous lesson, while the eyes seem to close, suddenly suggest: "Sleep—fast asleep," and sure the subject will fall into hypnosis.

LESSON 27.

HOW TO HYPNOTISE BY THE AID OF A BOOK.—Have your subject seated comfortably in a chair. Open at random any page of a book. Ask him to spell mentally every word of a line slowly and thus read the page. When he reads a few lines suggest: "You—will—sleep — before — you — finish — the — page; you — feel — sleepy; sleep—sleepy—sleep; your—eyes—are—closing; your—eyes—are — closing; sleep—sleep—have—your—

eyes—closed; your—eyes—have—closed; sleep — sleepy
—sleep—fast—asleep."

LESSON 28.

How to Hypnotise a Large Gathering at a Time.
—By the aid of any of the aforesaid three methods you
can hypnotise any number of persons at one and the
same time. When doing so it is preferable to ask them
to join their hands together. Make them stand or sit in
a semi-circle; in the meanwhile you should look them
in the face, so that each may be under the impression
that you are looking directly at him. This is the most
important thing you will have to pay particular attention to. If you have well mastered our exercise under
"Circular Influence" in Personal Magnetism you will be
astonished at the wonderful success you may achieve
now. After a few minutes you will see that their eyes
voluntarily close and at that time, say, when you count
three, they will be unable to open their eyes. You will
be astonished to see that they are mere automatons and
they are completely at your mercy. Mind you, take no
mean or undue advantage of that.

Another Method—Ask all the persons to think
firmly that they are going to sleep. You had better occupy a slightly elevated position so that all the persons
may have a look at you. Have your legs crossed one
over the other. Ask all the persons to look into your
eyes. Slightly waive your body to and fro and give a
rocking motion. Simultaneously have a slow rhythmic
music set up and die away in a few minutes. By the
time the music stops all the persons will be sound asleep.

LESSON 29.

How to Awaken Hypnotic Subjects.—Having
made yourself at home in the method of inducing hypnosis, you should carefully learn before experimenting
how to remove the influence. There is a knack required

to do this, and it can be acquired only by long practice.

To awaken a subject from hypnosis we give you the following methods after a careful investigation of the advantages and disadvantages resulting from such, and if you follow them strictly you will have no difficulty in your work.

1.   It is always better to put an end to Hypnosis by mental means, (i. e.) by the command to wake up at a particular signal. For example, if you wish to awaken a subject, suggest in a positive tone: "Now—when— I — count — three — you — will — awaken; ready — one — two — three — all — right — wake — up — wide —awake." You will see the subject usually awakens when you count three. You should give the subject ample time before giving suggestions for awakening. It is always better to give some such suggestions also as: "You — will — not — be — nervous — in — any — way; your—head—will—be—clear; you — will — feel — well," etc.

2.   THE UPWARD WAKING PASSES.—You should bear in mind that all downward passes tend to *produce* hypnosis, and all *upward* passes *dispel* the influence.

Place the palms of your hands together, with fingers spread out, and raise them rapidly in front of the subject, starting at the loins and going up along the outside of the arms to the cheeks, over the temples to the top of his head. Do this as though you throw air into his face and nostrils. Do this for 1 or 2 minutes and suggest in a positive tone: "All   right—wake   up—wide—awake." "All right—wake up—wide awake." As you give these suggestions clap your hands together sharply, about 4 inches from the top of the subject's head, until your subject is perfectly wide awake.

In a majority of cases it is found that when the subjects come out of hypnosis they usually smile. This is a clear indication of awakening. Sometimes, though your subject is awakened to all appearance, he would unconsciously relapse into hypnosis. Great care should be taken in watching the subject for a few minutes even after he has awakened. If it so happens, by any neglect, that he does not wake up, go through the awakening process again; you can easily understand by the facial expression whether he is in the normal state or in hypnosis. But as a rule hypnotists keep suggesting to their subjects: "All right—wake—up—wide—awake," etc., until they notice a smiling expression in the subject's face.

The effects of Hypnotism will completely wear off in time and a spontaneous awakening will usually occur without any bad results.

The clapping of hands may also be added to the first method.

There are some more methods of awakening. The following may also be adopted in addition to the above, and are, to a great extent, very efficacious.

1. The wafting an handkerchief rapidly before the subject's face produces a more rapid result than the upward passes.

2. By merely blowing cool breath or fanning over the head and face with a few transverse passes.

There are certain parts of the body where stimulation produces awakening. Among them the ovarian regions are particularly notable. This should not. in any consideration, be used except under very extraordinarily difficult cases. This is highly useful and essential for the student of Magnetic Healing.

4. *Forcible Means of Opening the Eyes.*—If the subject experiences a difficulty in opening his eyes, with the tips of your thumbs rub firmly and briskly (not thereby hurt him) over his eyebrows from the root of the nose outwards towards the temples and then fan a little. Within a very short time, say a minute, your subject will come to the normal wide awake state.

Fanning, excitation by the faradism, sprinkling with water, loud calls, etc., are hardly necessary, and we even think they are a little harmful.

INSTANTANEOUS HYPNOTISM.—Susceptibility of the subject can be increased when you get him into deep hypnotic sleep by telling him that in the future he will be very susceptible, that whenever you tell him to go to sleep he will at once fall into a deep sleep and you can hypnotise him immediately, etc. If such suggestions are repeated several times before awakening him they will produce a very strong impression on him. For instantaneous hypnotism it is not at all necessary that such precautious methods need be entered into. After a person has once been hypnotised, hypnosis can be brought forth almost instantaneously. Generally sudden hypnosis can be induced even in very first trials.

If the subject has never been hypnotised, it is always better to create a confidence in your ability by performing some simple test; for instance, fastening the hands together. In a vast majority of cases this will save a good deal of time.

Now, let your subject take a chair; carelessly pass by him once or twice and when right near him suddenly look into his eyes and tap him under his jaw with the first two fingers of your right hand At the same time suggest very emphatically and positively: "Your—tooth—is—aching; you—have—a—horrible—pain—you—cannot—bear—it; your—tooth—is—horribly—aching."

Suddenly you will see your subject jump with a horrible pain and at once suggest that the pain has entirely left him and immediately say: "Sleep—fast asleep."

ANOTHER METHOD.—This can be created generally with people who have once been under the influence of hypnosis; yet in many cases it succeeds wonderfully. Just when you hypnotise before an assembly try to catch hold of an youngster between 14 and 25 who might be putting on a thoroughly sceptic look. Just ask him to allow you to hypnotise him and when he comes near you, just walk towards him with a determined and commanding air and place one of your hands behind his neck and touch his chin sharply with the palm of the other hand. At once suggest: "Sleep; your senses are leaving you; the blood in your brains has come down; sleep quickly; fast asleep: you are going sound asleep." If this does not succeed, have him seated and pour on all the sleep formulæ without giving him time to think of any other thing.

How to Create Illusions and Hallucinations.— Sense delusions are divided into two kinds:

1. Hallucinations: ,The perception of an object where in reality there is nothing, is termed Hallucination.

2. Illusions: The false representation of an existing external object is called Illusion.

It is always easier to deceive the sense of taste than the sense of sight or hearing. A great care should be taken in making hallucinations, as it requires a very deep sleep. Hallucinations of sight are more easily caused when the eyes are shut. So if you wish to create any hallucination it is always better to tell the subject what you wish him to see before you have him open his eyes.

This should be well impressed upon the subject, and then suggest in a positive tone: "Open your eyes." The position best suited for this is to put the fingers of your left hand on top of subject's head and your left thumb on the root of the nose as you suggest. When his eyes are opened make a downward pass with your right hand, commencing above his eyes a little below the chin. It is better to say when giving such passes about the thing you wish him to see. If you fail in making the subject see what you wish, do not be discouraged. A simple insistence on your part that the object desired is before him will make the subject perceive it.

Any number of funs and jokes, inasmuch as they are within the bounds of decency, can be played out to your heart's content.

For example, hypnotise your subject and put him into a deep sleep. After allowing him a little time tell him that when he opens his eyes he will see a beautiful rose before him, and suggest to him to open his eyes and he will surely see the rose before him; if not, insist a little, and the desired effect will follow. You may then ask him to smell, eat, etc., or do anything with that imaginary rose, and he will surely do as you say. A careful attention should be given to the position you will have to occupy during such scenes.

LESSON 30.

In the same way, the states of Anæsthesia and Analgesia can be induced by mere suggestions.

How to Produce Anæsthesia and Analgesia.— Put your subject into a deep hypnotic sleep and suggest: "Your — leg — is — dead; there — is — no — feeling; you — will — suffer — no — pain." Repeat these 4 or 5 times positively, as you know suggestion takes effect by repetition. Now you can pass a needle or any pointed instrument through that part and you will find the subject insensible to both feeling and pain. Any kind of surgical operations can in this way be performed without the use of any narcotics or chloroform and without their resultant dangers.

It would also be better to suggest to the patient that his sleep is heavy and deep and he is growing unconscious. After a few suggestions take two small wire brushes connected with the poles of a battery and place the brushes over the supra-orbital nerves (just over the eyebrows); if he does not show any sensation of pain, you may safely perform any operation.

LESSON 31.

Hemi-Hypnosis.—An entire cessation of the functions of sense organs can be induced in the same way as hallucinations. Mere words, "You—cannot—hear; you —are—deaf; you—are—blind," suffice to deprive the hypnotic subject of the corresponding sense perceptions. In the same way a mere demand can restore the functions. Blindness and deafness can as well be created and even the sight of one eye can be prevented when the other can see as usual.

When the subject is properly hypnotised ask him to close his eyes or ears. Then suggest he can see with closed eyes or hear with closed ears. If a deep state of hypnosis is obtained the subject will, to the amazement of all, see and hear when the respective organs are closed.

LESSON 32.

CATALEPSY.—Ask your subject to stand before you, putting his heels together. Tell him to close his eyes and to make his body as stiff as possible. Then catch hold of the subject's neck with your left hand, just below where the head joins it. Put your right thumb on the right temple of the subject and your fingers on the temple. Let not the pressure be so hard as to cause any pain. Then say in a positive tone: "Sleep—sleepy—sleep — sound — asleep — sleep — sleepy — you — are —going — sound — asleep. You — will — not — fall; do — not — fear; your — body — will — remain — stiff — and — rigid; you — are — getting — sleepy — sleepy — sound asleep — fast — asleep." When you are satisfied that he is in deep sleep, say: "Your—muscles — are — getting — stiff — stiff — rigid — very — rigid — very — rigid." Repeat this four or five times. When you give these suggestions ask somebody to catch hold of the subject lest he should fall; make 4 or 5 downward passes with both hands over the shoulders down over the arms, and over the legs to the ankles; these passes should be made quickly. Then request some one to assist you in placing the subject across the back of two chairs of the same height. It would be better if some pillows are placed on the chairs, so as not to hurt or bruise the subject's flesh. The shoulders should be well on the back of one chair and the ankles may rest on the back of another. A great precaution should be taken in holding the chair:, so that they cannot move apart. It would be better if the subject is held. After keeping him in a horizontal position. raise him up in the centre and suggest: "Suff — rigid — very — stiff — stiff — very stiff — rigid — very — rigid; all — your — muscles — are — stiff — very — stiff; they — will — not — bend; but — your — heart — will — beat — normally." The body will be able to sustain a weight of 500 lbs., and this depends entirely upon your ability in making the body stiff. So it is better to first try the weight of one man and then increase it, if the subject seems to hold him all right. Under any circumstances do not keep the subject in this state very long.

How to Remove Catalepsy.—Do not keep the weight for more than a moment or two. Then take your subject from the chair, hold him well and suggest: "Your — muscles — are — getting — loose — loose; when — you — wake — up — you — will — feel — well; you —will — feel — quite — refreshed." Then awaken him by the regular process.

It is only very successful operators can undertake this test. This should not be undertaken to merely satisfy one's vulgar curiosity.

LESSON 33.

Power Over Animals.—Reader! you might have come across many who by a mere sign control the veriest and the wildest of animals, not only domestic but also w.ld. In Circus troupes and Menageries you have seen persons who play with lions, tigers, cheettahs, bears, wolves, etc.; do not be under the delusion that they are endowed with mystic or any superhuman powers. It is simply their magnetic gaze, fearlessness, and their knowledge of hypnotising animals; you can also become a controller of animals and this, in time, would save you from many a peril. A simple perusal of the following instructions will create a power in you by the aid of which you can command the animal realm.

We give you one or two sure methods of taming wild beasts. The general principle underlying the whole power is the acquisition of a magnetic gaze (which you have already acquired) and avoiding fear and rashness. Further, it would be better if you possess a little knowledge of the temperament and disposition of the whole animal kingdom.

How to Control a Horse—Go direct to the stable. Walk quickly and decidedly to the horse; keep close to his head. Do neither fear nor care if he roars or snaps at you. Boldly stretch out your right hand and catch hold of him by the forelock and then let your left thumb and forefinger close over his nostrils, and thus tighten your hold upon the septum or cartillage which divides the nostrils. Pull his head down and blow strongly. and steadily into his ear for five minutes. Then pat him gently on the shoulder and speak to him boldly and firmly as if you speak to a human being. Then make a few passes from between the ears down to the back as far as you can reach. In the meanwhile you should be very careful not to leave your hold on his nostril. Within a very short time you will see the most vicious of horses come completely under your influence. If it turns refractory even after this, do not fear. but boldly repeat the above process once or twice and you are sure to succeed as one and one is two.

How to Hypnotise a Guinea Pig.—Some animals if manipulated in certain peculiar positions can be thrown into a hypnotic state. The hypnotising of a guinea pig is of a very common method. Roll it over and over several times and lay it on its on its back; this will produce a dazed condition and the animal will fall into hypnosis, but its eyes will be almost open. Even by hanging it in abnormal positions hypnosis can be produced. A quick waving of the hand in front of its eyes or a noise will bring it back to the normal state.

How to Hypnotise Crocodiles and Alligators.— These can be very successfully and easily thrown into hypnosis. The procedure adopted is very simple. All

you have to do is to place them on the back and make
them remain in that state for a minute or two.

How to Hypnotise a Lizard.—This also is a very
simple task. All you have to do is to simply lay it on
its back and to prevent it from holding its jaws. You
must also be careful to catch hold of its tail for a time.

How to Hypnotise a Frog.—The method to be
adopted is as stated in the above case. This is a very
troublesome customer, and would require a longer time.

How to Hypnotise a Lobster.—What you have to
do in this case is nothing but to make it stand on its
head. It will within a very short time go into a sound
sleep.

How to Remove the Influence.—To bring these
creatures back to a normal state, simply blow sharply
on the nose for a few seconds and they will at once come
out of hypnosis.

How to Hypnotise a Hen.—Catch hold of it by
the neck; take a piece of chalk and have the head of
the hen slightly touching the ground and draw a line
with the chalk from its beak to some distance. You
may now safely leave it and it will not move an inch.
The curious fact with this creature is that it seems to
be under the impression that it has been tied with a
piece of thread or twine. Any sudden noise will bring
it back to the normal state.

All kinds of domestic animals can thus be brought
under your control except the dog, which does not require so much trouble on your part, but a steady gaze;
and it would not succumb to any other process. You
should bear in mind that the eye is the most powerful
agent in influencing animals.

When giving passes to animals give then steadily,
commencing over the eyes and down to the nostrils.
This will surely produce sleep in them. If they tremble,
it is a sure sign of success; calmly proceed with the

passes and do as if with a human being, with a firm determination in your mind. It is better to give short local passes over the eyes until they close of their own accord. After they have been hypnotised you can do whatever you please with them.

How to Remove the Influence.—Take your handkerchief, waft it rapidly over the animal and call out loudly; it will soon wake up.

How to Control Wild Animals.—This requires a long practice. It would be better if you can go to a menagerie and cultivate the art of arresting the attention of animals by your gaze. To control this class of animals it requires an extraordinary presence of mind, a firm, steady and unflinching gaze and knack which can be acquired only by long practice. If you acquire this, you can beard even the lion in its own den.

LESSON 34.

Post-Hypnotic Suggestions.—Post-hypnotic suggestions, or deferred suggestions, as they are called, are used with most gratifying results for the intellectual, ethical, moral and spiritual elevation of humanity. With the help of these we can completely change a person's disposition and nature. While in the hypnotic state, a subject will receive and accept any suggestions given him by the hypnotist which are not antagonistic to his religious or moral convictions, and he will act on them without any knowledge of the fact that they were given him by another.

For example, a boy who is disobedient disrespectful and perverse to study, etc., can be easily hypnotised and given post-hypnotic suggestions, which will completely change his nature and disposition, and make of him a perfect model of obedience and respect, and will also create an eager desire for study, etc., in him.

How to Give Post-Hypnotic Suggestions.—Put the subject in deep hypnosis. The deeper the sleep, the more sure the result will be. Take hold of his left by your right hand, as firmly as possible. Place your left fingers on the crown of the subject's head and tap slowly; during the operation suggest in a very positive tone: "When — you — wake up — you — will — take — my — dictionary — from — the — she'f — and — place — it — on — the — table; you — will — feel — an — inclination — to — do — so; you — cannot — resist — it; you — will — not — remember — that — I told — you — this; but — you — will — do — so." Repeat these suggestions five or six times, and as you give these suggestions look at the root of his nose with a great determination, that he will act up to your orders. Then awaken him as usual. Surely as soon as he awakens he will of his own accord do as you have asked him to do.

In the same way you can give suggestions to carry out anything, even after years together. When the appointed time comes he will naturally carry out your orders, without the slightest hesitation. Mind, your suggestions should not in any way be contradictory to his established views and principles.

Further, you should bear in mind, by the aid of these suggestions you cannot make anybody to do a Criminal Act; if you administer any such suggestions you will be sorely disappointed by a spontaneous awakening on the part of the subject and your influence will end therein, and you will be shunned and mistrusted by all. Further, this will cause in yourself a great block for the development of the higher and nobler phases of the science.

LESSON 35.

Hypnotising by Telephone Mail and Telegraph. —A great bait is thrown to you, Readers, and your mind is influenced by advertisements that you can in-

fluence people by Telephone, Mail, Telegraph, etc.   No
doubt this is true.   But you cannot hypnotise people
who have not been under your influence for a long time,
and it is only with such you can succeed.   The process
you have to follow is simply to speak or write some
"sleep suggestions," in bold characters, and despatch the
same to the party you wish to hypnotise.   You should
take great care in doing this.   Unless you are perfectly
satisfied that the party has been implicitly under your
influence and he can be thrown into hypnosis by a mere
word or look, and it is then and then only you can
adopt any of the above ways.

How to Influence People at a Distance.—This
is more or less a lessson under the power of Thought.
When that power has been well cultivated, this will be
mere child's play for you.   Hence we treat of this in a
more appropriate place in Telepathy.   When you have
finished this First Course you will simply marvel at the
wonders you work.

LESSON 36.

Hypnotizing in Natural Sleep.—Persons who are
refractory to hypnosis in their waking state can be easily
hypnotised when they are asleep.   For this, approach
the bed quietly and suggest in a very slow tone, almost
akin to a whisper.   "Sleepy — sleep — you — are —
sound — asleep; do — not — fear; you — must —
not — awaken; go — into — a — deep — sleep; sleepy
— sleep — sound — asleep."   This may be repeated
several times and then place your hand on his head and
say: "You — hear — no — voice — except — mine;
nothing — is — audible — to — you; you — are —
fast — asleep."   In the meanwhile before giving the
latter suggestions, if you find any signs of his awakening, quickly draw back and discontinue your work; if
not, proceed as instructed and after one or two minutes,
slightly ask him to smell, say "attar."   If he smiles

and enjoys the odor it is sure that he has come under your control. After finishing the work, if you do not wish him to remember that you have hypnotised him during his sleep, suggest that he will not remember what you have done when he awakens next morning. You may also first give one or two passes commencing at the top of his head down to region of heart. The passes should on no consideration be made "at contact." After having given a few passes you may give some suggestions and proceed as above.

LESSON 37.

TEST OF SLEEP.—It should not be confused that this is a special test for the above. It is not at all advisable to have recourse to this test when you hypnotise one in natural sleep. This is a general test. It is as follows:

After having followed any of the methods indicated in the course, for hypnotising, just suggest to the subject: "Your — arm — is — heavy; it — is — stiff — and — rigid; it — will — not — bend; you — cannot — bend — it." Then ask him to try and if you find him unable to do so, mind that he is well under hypnosis.

2. In the same way you can make one's pulse to beat slow or fast and if your orders are acted up, you may feel sure that the party is under hypnosis.

LESSON 38.

SPECIAL INSTRUCTIONS.—Reader, you have now become a practical Hypnotist. It is only a question of experience for you to become a thorough and an expert one. Under no circumstance blow your own trumpet; do not allow anybody to suspect by your actions that you are a Hypnotist and an influencer, unless you intend to become a professional Hypnotist. When you wish to Hypnotise anybody, do not try to put anyone to sleep until after you have exhibited a number of minor tests and dispelled the fear of hypnotism. Whenever possible, if you wish to treat your patient let your patient have the chance of seeing somebody hypnotised before him.   Make him feel at home, void of fear, anxiety and scepticism.   Remove all elements which may in any way tend to arouse or excite his mind. Everything you do must show that you understand your business perfectly well.   None of your actions should exhibit any timidity, bashfulness or half-heartedness.

LESSON 39.

ADDITIONAL METHODS FOR HYPNOTISING.—(a) Ask the subject to look directly at your eyes.   You must look at the root of his nose with a firm idea that he will fall into hypnosis soon.   When he looks at you command him to rotate his hands.   Speak to him rapidly or rather suggest the sleep formulæ and order him to increase the speed of rotation.   Within five or six minutes you will see that his eyes dilate, and then proceed for a short time more with the suggestions and he will soon fall into hypnosis.

(b)   Let the subject take a chair.   Ask him to close the holes of his ears by his fingers.   He will hear a sound as the falling of glass pieces, which will be of a quite musical nature.   After a few minutes suggest: "The noise is quite soothing; it produces a refreshing pleasant sensation in you; you are falling into sleep; sleep—sleepy—sleep—sound—asleep."

Any of the following properly applied will produce hypnosis:

(c)   Stimuli applied on the crown of the head.

(d)   A simple touching or stroking the forehead.

(e)   Any pressure on the cervical vertibræ.

(f)   A temporary cessation or stop of sense stimulation, e. g., closing of the eyes and a little pressure on the eyelids.

(g)   By presenting a Magnet.

(h)   A simple moving in a circle of one's head with a firm grasp on the back of the head by the left hand fingers, the right thumb at the root of nose and the other fingers on the right temple. A little inward and upward pressure at the base of the brain along with the above, will be more effectual. Sleep suggestions may also be given.

(i) Stimuli at corners of eyes, near root of nose when the eyes are closed.

(j) The application of a warm cloth at the pit of the stomach.

We are dicidedly of opinion that in each individual case the method should be selected by means of which the most vivid pictures of the hypnosis and the conviction that hypnosis will come on, can be impressed on the subject. We particularise "individual cases" because persons who appear refractory to one method will surely be influenced by another.

LESSON 40.

ADVANCED STAGES.

PARTIAL CLAIRVOYANCE.—After having put the subject into deep hypnosis, suggest: "Your soul is slowly coming out of your physical body; it is to take a short journey, leaving the body here; let it to go to (fix a place) and give me an account of all it sees." In course of time you will get accurate descriptions, though the versions are imperfect in the beginning. This is more or less Partial Clairvoyance. After you have finished the test suggest: "Your soul is now returning, let it enter your physical body." Give one or two minutes' time and then awaken the subject as usual.

LESSON 41.

HINDU LEVITATION.

LEVITATION.—Or raising the body in the air without any support. This can be done only by experts who have perfect control of their will. This more or less superhuman feat is done even at the present day by many in India. The *modus operandi* is as simple as anything; but the underlying principle, the power of the will, is no easy task. Ask your subject to lie prostrate on his back and induce as deep a hypnosis as possible. Then suggest mentally: "Your body will become filled with air; every portion of your body is charged with air; all the heavy components of your body will become as light as air." Then think firmly that his body will rise in the air. You may increase the height by continued practice. It is better if this test is practiced in low-ceilinged rooms. After a time suggest: "Your body is getting heavy as usual; you will slowly come to the surface of the earth; the components of your body slowly resume their usual weight, etc." This can also be practiced on yourself, when it is not necessary you must throw yourself in sleep. It is sufficient if you keep yourself in a perfect relaxed state and then take the above suggestions. Do not attempt this until you have developed your will power *perfectly*. It is better for the self practitioner of Levitation to first take in the undermentioned breathing exercise, which is naturally termed Pranayama. Close the right nostril with your finger and inhale air through the left for full sixteen seconds; then retain the air and close both the nostrils and be in this state for one full minute and four seconds; after that slowly expel the air retained through the right nostril. The expelling must occupy about 32 seconds. This whole process makes one Pranayama. The student must practice this until he is able to do one hundred pranayamas a day. The best time suited for the practice is the early morning before taking any food. This if practiced regularly will help the student a great deal in the process of Levitation.

LESSON 42.

SAMAHDI OR BURIAL ALIVE.

Samahdi or burial alive is the Hindu catalepsy. This is nothing but an advanced and improved stage beyond that of the ordinary catalepsy given in Lesson 22. This state can be induced both on yourself and in a separate subject. Spiritually it has been claimed to purify this physical body. When one is thrown into this super-human stage the heart action as well as the breathing completely stops. The subject can be buried or resurrected at the pleasure of the operator. It is only men who have succeeded in the previous one "Levitation" can undertake this feat. When the will has been properly trained the muscles will implicitly obey its commands. These advanced stages ought to be practically taken into the Advanced Course, but owing to the revision of our first edition and with a view to make ours pre-eminently the best one in the market, we have been forced to introduce these here. After throwing the subject into a cataleptic state give strong mental suggestions: "Your brain will lie dormant; all physical movements will cease; you will not breathe; your heart will not beat; you will remain in this condition for a week." Then force the tongue back into the mouth and fill the mouth, nostrils and all other cavities with wax, as ants, etc., are apt to destroy the body. Then bury the body. After the appointed time has expired as per above suggestions take the body out of the ground. In some cases as the fingers may become drawn straighten them out and remove the wax from the nose, the mouth and all other parts. Have the body well rubbed with oil and clean the cavities thoroughly with water. Then the mouth must be opened and air blown into it. The operator must determinedly with a great effort *will* that the subject must turn to the natural condition. You will see the muscles of the body slowly relax; and after a short time the breathing and the heart action will commence. The subject after an hour or so will slowly sit up. Then give him a *very light refreshment* in the beginning. Gradually he will turn out all right. We would caution you not to try this until you get an implicit confidence in your abilities and you chance to have an *expert* with you for assistance. You can also try this on yourself, but you must have someone by your side who is also well versed in this science to place you underground after well closing the cavities with wax. You must not undertake this till you have perfect control over your body and you have perfect success in Psychic Clairvoyance, or danger is sure to ensue. Do not be rash. Be careful.

CHAPTER III.

ANIMAL MAGNETISM.

LESSON 43.

MESMERISM.—The term Mesmerism was given to the practice of Animal Magnetism by the followers of Mesmer—and is now used to denote ordinary Somnambulism induced by artificial means. It is for all practical purposes a perfect form of Hypnotism.

And Hypnotism is a modern term suggested by Dr. Braid, and is synonymous to the former.

People generally confound mesmeric with hypnotic states, but each is distinct in itself, though apparently akin.

A little comment is necessary here to draw a clear outline between the two.

Hypnosis is produced by the combination of bright object and suggestion and passes, whereas Mesmeric sleep is induced only by passes. In hypnosis the mind of the subject slumbers. This dream life appears to him to be real waking normal activity. The life creations thus dreamed of are acted upon, with all earnestness. Here physical rather than mental phenomena are evolved; the states of Anæsthesia and Catalepsy are more or less present. The senses of smell and hearing are partially exalted and the subject is apt to be partially or fully unconscious. The respiration is frequently irregular, accompanied by slight convulsive movements.

(48)

Whereas in Mesmeric state the sleep is calm, refreshing, soothing and curative, the pulse is slow and rhythmic. The senses slumber and the mind awakens to a fuller independence and to the exhibition of several mental and spiritual powers not dreamt of hitherto. Here again the mind is exalted to such a degree as to attach a clearly defined hyper-sensuous condition paving a way for the seership, clairvoyance, clair-audience, thought-reading, etc.

As we go deeper into this state and investigate and research we are led to a clear understanding of the Soul apart from the phenomena induced by several pathological conditions of brain and body. The deeper the mesmeric sleep, the greater is the wakefulness and lucidity of the inner or soul life. And from practical research in this science we are of opinion that the nature and characteristics of the phenomena manifested are always consistent with the physical, mental, moral and spiritual nature of the operator in addition to those of the operated.

Our investigations along these lines lend us a high degree of seriousness and earnestness and we are literally thrusted into the spiritual realm. Further, the phenomena evolved during the development of this mighty and wonderful state are as the physical, mental and spiritual characteristics of the operator and the operated and more or less the same. Hence you should pay a careful attention to your life and restrict your habits to such a state as the strictest principles of moral code could not find the least fault.

With the above remarks duly presented we go direct into Mesmerism proper.

LESSON 44.

PASSES, AND WHAT THEY MEAN.—Mesmeric influence is generally carried out by the "gaze" and by "passes." You know how to gaze at anyone. Now you have to be initiated in the methods of giving passes. Passes are made "in contact" and "at distance."

How to Make Passes.—When you wish to make passes, raise your hands and move them downward with palms towards the subject from the top of the head down to the shoulders and leave them there about a minute, and then draw them along the arm to the extremities of the fingers, touching the subject lightly— "Passes at contact."

Place your hands upon the subject's head; hold them there a moment and bring them down before the face, at the distance of one or two inches, as far as the pit of the stomach; there let them remain about 2 minutes. passing the thumb along the pit of the stomach and the other fingers down the sides. Then descend slowly along the body as far as the knees, or farther; and, if you can conveniently, as far as the ends of the feet.— "Passes at distance."

In making passes you should always use the thumb and three fingers of each hand; also that part of the palm which would remain if the little finger and part of the hand were cut off from between the little and and third finger to the wrist. The ends of the fingers should be a little curved. In "Passes at contact" the pressure should be light. Different kinds of passes will be treated under "Magnetic Healing."

These can be easily cultivated. You should bear in mind that they are not only the pantomime language of the will but they are the vehicle to convey some magnetic fluid from you to the subject. The passes you give should be performed in calm, easy, graceful and natural way. No physical strain or exertion is necessary, but a mental activity. This art can be easily cultivated. At times you should be prepared to make passes even for a period of one full hour without the least semblance of physical weakness on your part.

LESSON 45.

How to Produce Mesmeric Sleep.—Ask your subject to lie down upon a sofa or on an easy chair. Stand by his side, with a determined will that he will go asleep, make passes "at distance," commencing from the crown of the subject's head down over the face, the body and thence to the knee. Then slightly press his knees with the middle fingers of your hands for a few seconds—say 5. Then repeat the same until you perceive the dropping of the subject's eyelids and the resultant sleep state. Let each pass occupy 3 minutes. Generally it takes about 20 or 30 minutes to bring one to the mesmeric trance.

Ask the subject to lie on a couch. Tell him to inhale and exhale as slowly as possible. When he is so doing make a few passes over the face and breast. Almost all the subjects will fall into deep hypnosis within 15 minutes at the most.

We can explain a dozen other methods for producing mesmeric trance, but the two given here are pre-eminently the best. We do not know of any other that compares with these in any way. To say the least, these are the methods adopted by all leading Mesmerists of the day.

The way to get your subject out of trance is the same as was referred to under hypnosis, and as such it requires no repetition here.

But some use passes what are called "Demesmerising passes." The way of administering these passes is to commence from the toes and go backwards to the crown of the head and throw off the hands. This method is also very effective.

LESSON 46.

Suggestive and Psycho-Therapeutics.—Our instructions in Suggestive Therapeutics cover also all the phases of Psycho-Therapeutics; and it is needless on

our part to treat them separately. You will clearly understand Psycho-Therapeutics as you handle Suggestive
Therapeutics.

Before you proceed any further in these branches of
science, it is absolutely necessary for you to know something about mind and its power over the body, as
Psycho-Therapeutics is no other than Mind or Mental
Healing.

All Mental Scientists agree that the mind is twofold
in its nature. Mind is made up of several faculties, of
which some are called the "Objective" and some "Subjective." Let us now enquire what the "Objective" and
"Subjective" minds are.

THE OBJECTIVE MIND.—The Objective Mind is the
ordinary, normal, wideawake mind, which you are using
now as you read these words. It is the mind which
makes you conscious of all that is going on around
you, and with which you work every day. This is your
tool or weapon for making your way in the world;
rather it is your "Outer Shell."

THE SUBJECTIVE MIND.—And the Subjective Mind
or Sub-Conscious Mind, as it is otherwise called, is the
store-house for the experiences and impressions of the
Objective Mind. It is the most active when you sleep.
Dreams come from the Subjective Mind. It never for-
gets anything. It records each and every trifling experience of your lifetime. It is absolutely receptive to
impressions from the Objective Mind. Whatever you
believe with your Objective or Reasoning Mind will be
recorded as a fact by your Subjective Mind. The Subjective Mind is "You" or your "Self." It is your character. It can be moulded *ignorantly* and *thoughtlessly*,
or with *wisdom* and *forethought*. *You can make your
Character what you will; therefore you can make your
life what you will.*

Apart from the nature of this faculty of mind, already
described, there is one more important aspect of the

mind which deserves special attention on the part of the student of Suggestive and Psycho-Therapeutics; i. e., *the Subjective Mind absolutely controls the involuntary bodily actions,* such as the heart's action, the digestive process, the automatic or involuntary movements of the eyelids, lungs and limbs. Remember then that control of the Subjective Mind means control of the health of the body.

LESSON 47.

SUGGESTIVE THERAPEUTICS.—Suggestive Therapeutics is specially adapted to diseases of a functional and nervous character, but it may be used in the treatment of all human ailments. It can never, in any case, produce the slightest harm if properly administered. Some are of opinion that it is necessary to get the patient into a deep sleep, before treating him by the Suggestive Therapeutics; but on the contrary, we have found from actual experience that it is not entirely so. A patient might also be cured in his waking state by employing suggestions. It does not matter in any way whether your patient goes to sleep or not, but give your suggestions just the same as if he were in deep hypnosis. Suggestion will take effect in the waking state in due time. This is a very important point to which you should pay particular attention. *It should be remembered that suggestion oversteps the bounds of medical treatment and trenches on the field of Psychology.* If suggestion is to succeed, the patient must firmly believe he will be cured. This belief must be impressed upon him, as an idea implanted in hypnosis takes a deep root. We think that hardly any of the newest discoveries are so important to the art of healing, apart from surgery, as the study of suggestion. Suggestion sets the conscious will in the right direction as the education does. As suggestion is the basis of the above two sciences, your suggestions must be specific in their character, and as you give your suggestions, put your hands on that portion of the patient's body in which the disease is located. Gently massage the affected parts. whenever you give a patient suggestions to counteract the nature of his disease, always be positive in giving utterance to such suggestions. You know already that one of the *secrets of success in life consists in being able to give strong, well formed suggestions.* Remember, that positive suggestions carry much weight; produce astounding results; influence people; effect astonishing cures, and they are a power in every walk of life. Therefore, to be an expert in giving positive suggestions with force, practice until you are able to attain that stage. In making verbal suggestions it would be very useful for you to note the following hints:

Do not speak loudly or drawl your words. Give the suggestions in a low voice positively and with the force of character. You may think that to speak positively means you must speak loudly; but we tell you that you may speak positively even in whisper. Do not, however, whisper in giving suggestions to the patients, but give them in a milder voice. Try various tones upon a friend, and ack him which tone seems to affect him most. By this method you can very successfully get the proper knack in giving suggestions. In treating patients the following rules should specially be followed:

1. Avoid continuous stimulation of the senses as much as possible.

2. Avoid all mentally exciting suggestions.

3. Do away with the suggestions carefully before awakening.

LESSON 48.

We now give you a method to treat a person without putting him to sleep.

How to Treat a Patient Without Putting Him to Sleep.—Ask the patient to lie down on a sofa; tell him to close his eyes, and request him to attend carefully to what you say and think upon it. In treating

a patient for any form of disease, make it a point
always to have him close his eyes and request him to
implicitly obey your instructions.   For it has been
found by long experience that it is very easy to cure
one with his eyes closed, as his mind is in a better
receptive condition to accept the statements.   Then tell
him to try to go to sleep and it is better for you to suggest him then these words: "Sleep—sleepy—sleepy—
fast asleep—sound asleep," etc.   After some time make
a series of long passes over him and then suggest him
in a low but positive tone, taking care in employing
suggestions to counteract the symptoms of the disease.
Repeat the suggestions several times.   This treatment
should be given once or twice a day, until you completely eradicate the disease of the patient.   In giving
suggestions, be sure to use such language as would be
intelligible to the patient and make your suggestions
specific in character, so as to suit each patient whom
you may have to treat.

Converse freely with the patient. and get all possible
details of his ailment from him. Examine his tongue
carefully and see whether it is free from all kinds of
precipitates, etc., what the disease is, and treat as per
instructions.

All kinds of bad and evil habits, such as liquor habit,
tobacco, smoking, snuff, chewing, morphine habit,
opium, biting the finger nails, etc., can be cured in one
or two treatments.   There are a number of other habits
which might be mentioned here, but we feel the above
sufficient.

Perverted sexual desires, perverseness to study, etc.,
may be relieved in the same way.   In fact, any habit—
it makes no difference what it is—can be cured by suggesting to the patients that they will have no desire to
do what they have been doing, etc., giving them suggestions for their particular habit.   It is not necessary
for you to follow the suggestions we give you.   All that
is necessary to say to the patient is what you wish to
accomplish.   Habits are purely mental diseases.   There

is no other more efficacious treatment for disease of this kind than suggestions. If you will study this lesson very carefully you will be able to cure the most obstinate habits in a very short time. Should you desire for more information in regard to any special habit, we will be pleased at any time to give you the specific way of treatment. You cannot conceive of the vast number of diseases you can immediately and effectively cure by the aid of hypnotism until you have had an actual experience in them.

As far as our experience permits we shall give you a few of the diseases that are curable by the aid of this branch of science.

Particularly suitable ones are all kinds of pain which have an anatomical cause (headaches, stomachaches, ovarian pains, neuralgic and rheumatic pains, even with effusion in joints, but we must not confuse with hysterical effusions); sleeplessness, hysterical disturbances; particularly paralysis of the extremities and aphonia; hysterical vomiting, polyuria, disturbances of menstruation; spontaneous somnambulism; uneasy dreams; loss of appetite; vomiting pregnancy; alcoholism; morphanism; nicotinism; nervous asthma; stammering; chronic constipation; nervous ocular disturbances; nocturnal emissions; incontinence of urine; pruritus of the skin of nervous origin; sexual perversion, if not congenital; ringing in the ear; writer's cramp; vaginismus; chorea, especially if the cause is psychic; paramoclonous; the neuroses of traumatism and emotions; agraphobia and obsessions.

As the suggestions only vary as to the nature of diseases we have refrained from giving the suggestions also, lest the course would become a ponderous one. *In methodical suggestion lies the key to Suggestive Therapeutics.* Just as suggestion can take away pain, it can create and strengthen it. When the hypnotised subject refuses the suggestion, which sometimes happens, no therapeutic result will be obtained. Hypnotism does not necessarily succeed at once. If the hyp-

nosis is deep, a result may be very quickly obtained.
Sometimes the object of treatment can best be obtained
by pursuing a slightly round-about way. Persons have
been weaned from bad habits like tobacco, etc., not by
direct command, but by suggesting that the smell of the
tobacco is unpleasant. In other cases we have found it
an excellent plan to place the hypnotic subject back
into earlier periods of life.

We have sometimes been unable to remove acute pain
even during deep hypnosis. But if we placed the patient
back in a period when he suffered no pain, it has been
possible in many cases not only to remove the pain
during hypnosis, but to find that it does not return on
awakening.

Great care should be taken in frequent repetition of
the suggestion during hypnosis, and its communication
in a present, not a future, form.

In some cases patience and method are wanted, and
the time the illness has lasted must be taken into consideration. The more the idea of pain has taken root,
the more difficult it is to overcome. Patience on the
side of both Doctor and Patient is often required.

SELF-CURE BY AUTO-HYPNOSIS, OR, EVERY MAN HIS
OWN HEALER.—All diseases can be cured by what is
known as auto-suggestion given by your active to
passive mind. The very habit of making the passive
mind amendable to the commands of the active function
might have been acquired by you. The curing by auto-
suggestion is good, as you simply keep on repeating to
the passive mind the statement that the new habit exists
(ignoring the old one), and the passive mind, although
inclined to be a little rebellious at first, will eventually
accept what you say as truth. Auto-suggestion is practically self-hypnosis of the passive mind by the active
mind. For example, if you have a pain in any part of
your body—say your leg—the safe way to cure it by
mental healing is by writing on a slip of paper some
similar suggestion: "I have no pain; my leg does not
hurt me; I am quite well; there is nothing the matter

with me; I will be quite well." These suggestions can be made in the waking state just as well as in the sleeping stage. The best time to take auto-treatment is at night after you retire to bed. When you begin to feel drowsy, concentrate your mind upon the suggestions: "Tomorrow when I awaken, I will feel better; the pain in my leg will completely leave me; I will be quite well." Make up your mind, without allowing other thoughts to enter, that the results will be satisfactory, that each day you will improve; that you will feel better in every way. It is also a good plan to lie down once or twice during daytime, too, and repeat such suggestions as you wish.

AUTO-HYPNOSIS.—Retire into a quiet room; lie or sit in a convenient position. Relax all your muscles perfectly. Look intently at the tip of your nose. In a short time you will fall into a deep hypnosis.

ANOTHER METHOD.—Take an easy position in a chair or a lounge, or better still, on a couch. Then roll the tongue towards the uvula and partially close the eyes. And within an incredibly short time you will go into a deep sleep. This is one of the best methods that was in vogue among the practitioners of Hatha Yoga in India.

As an aid to improve your health and vigour, we give you here certain well formed suggestions, and if you will repeat them as in the above process you will certainly be endowed with perfect state of health and vigour. Repeat mentally: "I am feeling better; I will soon be well; I will not allow any disease to exist in my body; I will be perfectly cheerful and healthy." If you do this, you will be surprised at the result obtained. This same rule applies to strengthening the memory, increasing the power of concentration, developing Personal Magnetism, or avoiding any bad habit which you wish to get rid of. Write to us if you require our assistance in acquiring any of the above said things; we will surely help you with detailed instructions to achieve your end. It is not necessary for you to undergo any of the so-called memory training systems. You may easily cultivate a good memory in you as well as in others by simple auto and common suggestions.

Bear in mind, by repeating mental exercises you can develop any faculty you desire, and if you will experiment with this you will soon be able to cure yourself of any disease. Consider you cannot cure yourself of a deep rooted habit or a chronic disease in a day. It usually requires some weeks—two or three. It depends mainly upon your power of concentration and force of will.

People who are the happy possessors of the power of going to sleep at their will, need never suffer from insomnia, besides being able to alleviate many pains to which the flesh is heir.

Those who follow the above instructions in all candour enthusiastically and determinedly will reap a abundant reward for their labour.

CHAPTER IV.

MIND READING.

LESSON 49.

Mind Reading is the act of transmitting or receiving thought and this is generally confused with Muscle Reading. The latter is a separate and different branch, of which we treat in the following. This branch is the stepping-stone and basis to that highly developed faculty —the Mind Reading or Telepathy.

The previous training you have had in this Course, though not essential, yet you will find it to be of great use in mastering this much talked of branch.

The principle underlying Muscle Reading is physical contact, whether by hand, by chord or by wire; whereas, in Mind Reading the action is not physical, but is purely a mental one, and its principle is the transmission of thought without physical contact, or musculation, as it is called, and without the agency of the five senses.

Having laid before you the nature of the two branches of Mind Reading, we shall now proceed to treat them separately in detail.

You are now ready to engage literally in a process of education—the education of a sense apart from the five acknowledged—the Thought—the sixth important sense. You should slowly develop this wonderful branch and should not all of a sudden expect too much. Do not be discouraged if you fail in one or two attempts.

(60)

"Rome was not built in a day;" "Patience and Perseverance overcome mountains." Persevere and we are sure you will succeed as others have done. Remember that all successful Mind Readers have stepped into the pedestal of renown, not all of a sudden, but by years of patient study, experiments and perseverance. Once you have accomplished successfully a few feats, you will never consent to part with the power for any consideration.

Remember that "Thought tends to take form in action" is one of the great truths of Mental Science. You may observe this in your daily life if you only care for it. For instance, if you clearly observe the gestures which accompany the mental conditions of fear, joy, grief, satisfaction, anger and surprise, etc., of a man, you will be astonished at the fact that the gestures which follow the condition of mind will be correspondingly automatic. Such a gesture is unconsciously the corresponding form of the then condition of the mind. The secret you learn from the above is that the man who tests the muscle reader innocently and unconsciously helps him by an automatic action or unconscious muscular activity.

To become an adept in Muscle Reading, first of all you should learn "how to relax" your muscles. Many persons believe that they can completely relax themselves when they cannot actually do so. If you have not this ability it is well that you should find it at once, so that you can practice until you are able to do so and attain passivity, because it means very much for your success in this science.

LESSON 50.

How to Perform the Test of "Relaxation."— Retire into a quiet room, seat yourself conveniently in a chair, place your left forearm upon the tip of the right hand pointer and let the full weight of the hand rent upon the finger, using it as a means of support merely.

Then count, One—two—three, and immediately you count three, remove the finger very quickly. If you have relaxed the muscles completely the arm of its own accord will fall into your lap as your finger is removed, just as a book placed on the finger would fall down when the support is removed. If your hand should not fall, it is clear that you have not complied with our instructions, that is, you have not relaxed your muscles. If you fail in your attempt, read the instructions clearly once more and try hard until you succeed. Generally a second trial will crown you with success. The left hand must not be pushed or forced into your lap, but all the muscles in the left hand and arm should be completely relaxed or loosened, when it would fall down as a dead, inert body.

Here we give you our tests to practice and experiment in Muscle Reading, and if you follow them diligently you will undoubtedly become a successful Muscle Reader.

In undertaking the following tests it is best to have a number of people present. You must not attempt too many experiments at a time. Further, the duration of the experiments also must be short and limited.

LESSON 51.

Retire into a room and ask one of your friends who is not aware of the principles of Muscle Reading to blindfold you with a kerchief and request him to hide anything, such as a knife, holder, pencil, etc., in a well concealed place within the room. Now, after he has concealed the thing tell him: "My friend, one thing I wish to instruct you for the successful practice of the test, and that is, you must first lend me your hands, keep your whole attention fixed upon the place where the knife is hidden, then upon the knife itself; I think I will be able to find out the knife." Then take hold of his right hand in your left and completely relax or loosen all the muscles of your hand and be ready to observe even the least motion or vibration of his hand. In case you do not notice any such movements of his hand, suggest to him excitedly: "Think, my friend, think, keep your mind well upon the place and think only of the spot where the knife lies." Immediately after move a step forward. You do this only with an effect to make the guide impart a vibratory motion unconsciously to your hand, which is a sure and sufficient clue to allow yourself moving along that direction. These vibrations or muscular movements may take two forms in the beginning. It may be a slight obstructive or check motion of his hand, that is a pull back which clearly testifies to you that the direction along which you proceed is wrong, or it may be a strong and firm leading on of your hands and supporting you with all his possible unconscious help. In either case, the muscular movement of your friend's hand is your key and leading instrument to the place where the knife is. Bear in mind, now, the more intense is the concentration of his mind upon the knife, the more you are sure to succeed in finding it out, and the more he is absorbed in the performance of his duty in good faith, the more unconscious material help you will have.

Now, if you notice "a leading on of your hands," simply follow the direction, and when you reach the place where the knife is hidden, you will observe the check motion (already mentioned) or unusual greater resistance of his hand to continue any further. At that time stop all of a sudden, pass your hands on the ground and sure you will closely locate the article and thereby find out the knife.

LESSON 52.

How to Find Out a Concealed Pin When You Are Blindfolded.—A somewhat similar method is adopted in finding out a pin or the whole in which it has been kept. To make the experiment easy of accomplishment and to attain greater success with ease, it is better to have two guides instead of one. Request them to encircle your neck with their four hands so that the thumbs of the hands of each guide touch each other, and the little fingers of each hand of the one touch those of the opposite hands of the other. By this you have the benefits of two concentrated minds and you can receive plenty of impulses and nerve indications "for a move."

Step by step move as you are guided by the unconscious action of the guides.

As you near the place where the object is hidden, you will receive a "distinct" impulse directing you to stop. It may be possible then for you to notice by feeling a gentle downward pressure on your shoulders instructing you thereby to stoop down and stretch out your arms for picking up the object. Here is a thing worth noting for you. Just as you stretch your arms upon the "object" you may not be sure that that object was the one chosen; and to assure you that that was the one in search, you may notice the greetings or loud exclamations of your audience. Upon this take it up and loudly and cheerfully give out to the audience: "Here is the thing you wanted me to find out."

By these cautious movements your audience will be greatly pleased and gratified, and they will unconsciously aid you in your further experiments. This test must be tried a number of times with varied articles until you become perfectly acquainted with the movements of the muscle.

LESSON 53.

How to Ascertain a Note or a Key of a Piano Thought of.—The secret of picking out certain notes or keys on a piano is very similar to the Exercises 1 and 2. To guide you along your work, relax all the muscles of your right hand and then take hold of his left hand by your right. Move your left hand quickly from one end to the other of the piano. At the same time move to and fro your right hand. If you do like this your friend will involuntarily hesitate somewhere; then you may stop and move your left hand over a very limited space until you finally settle upon the exact spot.

LESSON 54.

How to Write the Name Thought of.—This is a most difficult experiment, and it should be undertaken by the student only after he has become an expert. Provide yourself with a blackboard or any black surface. Take hold of his left hand by your right. Hold a chalk in your left hand and mark out lines in the shape of movements of his hands on the blackboard. These scribblings may, after due practice, take a rational form, that is, in the form of some characters. The automatic movements are unconsciously the then symptoms of a mental causation on the part of your friend. If you but clearly watch the voluntary movement of your friend's hand and if you write on the board corresponding vibratory movements of your right hand, you are sure to reproduce the mental assertion of your friend in the form of words. Your friend whose thought you are reading will assist you without knowing he is doing so.

Several other feats may thus be performed by you with complete success with a little prudence and diligence. When you meet with difficulties be sure to write to us and we will explain and give you an earnest help.

To find an article, number, or do a certain thing, it is necessary for you to give prompt obedience to the indications given you. The concentration of attention necessary for you can only come by practice. A lot of astonishments and amusements will follow if your friend honestly concentrates his mind upon the things to be done. Implicitly follow our instructions. You will be astonished at the miraculous wonders you will be able to do.

CHAPTER V.

TELEPATHY.

LESSON 55.

The sending and receiving of thought messages in the form of words or pictures without the assistance of the five senses is called Telepathy. Thought passes from mind to mind through the great ethereal ocean of communication between place to place. It is an electrical movement originating in the brain or gray matter and vibrating the ether. *Thought is not only a dynamic force but is a real thing as any other material object.* We cannot smell or taste thought, as we do not smell or taste the pure air. Thought sends out vibrations as light and heat do, but they are of a higher intensity. The chief usefulness of this science is that, however the distance may be, it in no way interferes either in projecting or receiving thoughts. You must not hurry over the practice, nor be eager enough to be a master of both time and space within a day. It is only practice that makes man perfect. When just once you have taken the study of this wonderful and interesting science you will never be satisfied to leave it alone, until you have become a perfect master of it. Of course there are people who can more easily project and receive thoughts than average men, but this can be attained by everyone who is willing to try it. So thought waves can be directed as well as received if sufficiently practiced.

(66)

Easy tests should at first be tried and gradually worked up to more difficult tests. The secret of success is earnest expectation. If you fail in the beginning do not be discouraged, but keep at it until you get good results and work smoothly. A proper training with the following exercises will make you an expert in Telepathy and will develop in yourself a confidence and aid you in acquiring the knack of sending out thought messages. You should do this for the sake of practice, and practice alone, and not merely for your amusement, and never for the amusement of your friends. You should never trifle with the mighty forces or exhibit them to satisfy the vulgar curiosity of others. When you have grasped the real significance of the law of mental control you will have no desire to parade your knowledge. On the other hand, you should keep continuously practicing with the firm understanding that you are paving a way to a higher use of your growing power.

This branch requires the aid of a friend, and it would be advantageous if he is one with whom you have practiced the exercises in Muscle Reading, or better if he himself is a practitioner of the science itself. As the practice requires a Projector as well as a Receiver, you may take whatever position you please, as success in either of them is gratifying. No doubt the position of the Receiver is a difficult one, requiring great tact and patience, so we give you instructions assuming that you take the position of a Receiver. Before taking any other tests please practice the following exercises, as they would show you what Thought can do.

LESSON 56.

When you go down a street, direct your attention upon some person walking just ahead of you within a distance of 10 feet or more and "will" firmly that he shall turn his head and look around in your direction. Your gaze should be focussed at the back of his neck just at the base of the brain. After a little practice you will get the required knack and you will be surprised at your success. Women are more susceptible to this mental influence than men. You may as well multiply the exercise by your own ingenuity and practice thoroughly.

LESSON 57.

Take a person who is sitting in an opposite row, not directly opposite to your position but a little towards the right or the left. Look direct opposite to you, so that if the person turns around he may not see that you are looking at him, and look at him through the corners of the eye. Think firmly that he will turn in the direction you are sitting and in a short time towards yourself; then direct the magnetic gaze in his face. It will produce a good effect.

LESSON 58.

Just when you pass in the roads turn your look towards any person, either going before you or approaching you; will firmly that he will turn either to the right or left and you will find that he unconsciously acts to your orders. If these exercises are well practiced you may perform wonderful feats.

Now to our regular work of a Receiver. As instructed above you must have a lot of patience. Both of you, you and your friend, must proceed with a firm determination to succeed in your efforts. Confidence is the greatest factor to be considered.

LESSON 59.

Have your friend take a seat in one end of a room and seat yourself in the other end. If you do not chance to have any screen or obstruction, etc., between you, have your eyes blindfolded. Let your friend take any article and look at it firmly; hold his attention to it; think that you will understand what it is. It is better if he looks at the article through a funnel or a tube made of paper (wide at one end and narrow at the other), as his attention will not then be drawn towards any other thing. In the beginning it would be better if you have many persons to look at the object through the tubes and all of them think that you will know what it is. After a short practice you may dispense with the services of all except your friend. This experiment must be tried with various objects. During the trials you must keep yourself in a perfectly relaxed state, ready to receive any impression that may come to you. You must in no way guess or conjecture the object. Your conjectures will mislead you a great deal and baffle your improvement. Ten minutes is sufficient for a single object. If you do not receive any impression, desist from practice that day. Do not verify your impressions at once. Have them all written. At the close of the experiments verify them, and some may prove to be right and some wrong. Do not grow disgusted. You cannot master this wonderful power in an hour. Patiently proceed with the exercises day by day, and in course of time you will be able to decipher all impressions very accurately.

LESSON 60.

Now ask your friends to think of a number, preferably below ten in the beginning, and then increase the digits. It would be better if they have it written on a piece of paper and proceed as above. After a short practice you will be able to give out very accurately the numbers thought of.

LESSON 61.

Let your friends think that you will do a certain action—say that you will enter into a room and go towards a table and take a book that is kept on it and bring it to the place they are. Blindfold your eyes and let one of your friends lead you into the room and leave you there. Let them all firmly think that you must proceed step by step. They must all be looking at you, and if you find anything in your way or go towards anything that may impede your progress they must warn you. Or even if you are wrong—say, swerve towards any wrong direction or go beyond the fixed place—they must all firmly think that you are wrong. You must very cautiously and slowly proceed step by step and thus always wait for the impressions you may receive. When you have approached the table they must firmly will that you must stretch your hand, lower it, or raise it, as required, and take hold of the object. Thus after every action your friends must will firmly of the subsequent action. After you have well succeeded proceed to the following.

LESSON 62.

Now take one selected friend and proceed with this exercise. It would be better if you often change the Projector, as it would facilitate to receive various impressions that may vary in their intensity. You must not confine yourself to only one friend. Concentrate your mind on a friend who is at a distance and think that he will write to you on a certain date. He will surely do so. It would be better in the beginning if you take someone with whom you are in correspondence. Then will that he will write on a certain definite subject. When you have attained satisfactory progress, try this with persons whom you know but with whom you have no correspondence.

LESSON 63.

How to Send Out a Telepathic Message to Your Friend at a Distance.—Suppose you wish to intimate your friend at a distance a thought message, you should write out the message on a sheet of white paper and then intently look upon the suggestions. To assist you in concentrating your vision it is advisable to have a simple instrument constructed on a large sheet of paper. Take a large sheet of paper and roll it in the form of a funnel, 2 feet long and 4 inches in diameter, broad at one end and narrow at the other. Now place the paper with the message before you upon a table. Sit near it in a chair and hold the funnel (broad end) to your eyes. This is done merely for the purpose of shutting from your view the surrounding objects and to assist you in the concentration of your vision upon the message. By looking at it constantly you will see the message growing dim and indistinct. But do not allow such a thing to take place; by moving the pupils of the eye to and fro within the range of the paper you can avoid such. In this experiment the eye should not be allowed to grow fatigued. In case it shows any such fatigue, you should wink your eyes as often as possible. If you practice this exercise daily with previous notice to your friend, regarding the time of exercise, he will surely record very correctly your message.

By the aid of Telepathy people even at a distance of 500 to 1,000 miles can be influenced without any trouble whatever. Suppose you wish to have an interview with a stanger and to interest him in your plans and enterprises, you may influence him by the method already explained. To do this it will be better to go into a quiet room and either lie or sit down in an easy-chair and entirely relax your muscles and keep yourself in a state of passivity and also shut out all disturbing thoughts and think intently but calmly of the person whom you wish to influence. The eyes should be closed and the effort must be calm and steady and you may get a mental image of the person. If you have never seen the person before, make the figure mentally without any distinct features. When this stage is attained, repeat mentally what you wish to do and imagine him doing as you wish. Your thought waves will reach your man with the greater force and do the needful. This requires a great practice.

THE END OF BOOK ONE.

INDIA'S
HOOD UNVEILED

SOUTH INDIA MYSTERIES

Book Two

INDIA'S
HOOD UNVEILED

SOUTH INDIA MYSTERIES

Book Two

HINDU HYPNOTISM, MESMERISM, CLAIR-
VOYANCE AND TRANCE

PRACTICAL INSTRUCTIONS
HOW TO DEVELOP AND EMPLOY
OCCULT AND SPIRIT POWER

BY A NATIVE OF
SOUTH INDIA

Published exclusively in the United States by

THE de LAURENCE COMPANY
Chicago, Ill., U. S. A., 1910

Preface to Book Two

This work is an endeavour to instruct you how to awaken and set at work the dormant faculties of your brain, that you may be able to overcome all undesirable conditions now existing, and to start into operation the hidden forces of your being which will give your life a new and inspiring measure.

In beginning I wish to tell you that *Man is not the weak worm of the dust* that he has always supposed himself to be, but that he is a God, through which the God-mind manifests and externalizes itself.

You at the present moment have Power, Strength, Wisdom and Intelligence, existing in your sub-consciousness of which you are unaware. Moreover, you have these attributes in all the quantities and qualities that you will ever need or desire.

All that is necessary for you to do to manifest these desirable conditions is a belief, a faith in the mighty truth just stated to you. You may learn just how to draw upon these hidden forces of your being and by that means demonstrate the truth of my assertion.

As a beginning, I shall demand that you cease denying the truth of all things which you at the present stage of your mental development do not entirely understand and know to be the facts.

Hitherto you only acknowledged the truths demonstrated to you by means of your five senses, viz., seeing, hearing, tasting, smelling and feeling; but you will soon

(77)

learn to know that you have other senses which may be called into action at will.

Your Super-conscious Mind is the God of the Universe and is All-powerful. All-knowing. This life within you is your real self. It is the as-yet-unexpressed self, in which you "live, move and have your being." When you refuse this understanding of God and refuse to believe it is the hidden power within you— you limit your physical strength and power to do or to be.

It is not my purpose to teach you something you do not know, but to teach you something you already know, but do not know that you know it. All knowledge exists in the sub-conscious mind of man and may be drawn upon without limit.

Man's first duty to himself and to humanity is to seek the powers which are latent within himself. These dormant faculties of the brain, when found, must be used and developed. By the use of these latent faculties man will discover the power to add to himself whatever he desires, whether that be the attainment of spiritual knowledge, health, wealth, friends, position or happiness in any of its phases.

The directions herein are an endeavour to arouse you to the truth of what you can do for yourself and explain how to proceed, promising that the result will be health, prosperity, friends, position and all else that is good.

There is no royal road to learning. There is only one way to know a thing and that is through experience which is the result of trial. The best that we can do with regard to what other men know is to assume their statements to be true, and then find out some way to test the truth of such statements by trial.

To accomplish all that is held out to you, you must begin with the assumption that all the potentialities that exist, exist in you. You must assume to be true that the *Kingdom of God* is within you and that this Kingdom is your real self and able to add to you all things whatsoever you may desire.

The most powerful suggestion that I may give you is *"All the power necessary to bring you the good there is in life, is in you."* I do not claim for myself a single virtue or power that I do not concede to all others; nor do I concede to any other a virtue or power that I do not claim for myself. ¡The sooner you recognize these truths the sooner you will be free. The time is now.

At the present time there has been formulated and adopted concise rules by which the working principles have become practical and applicable to all those whose unfolding minds are ripe for their revelations.

The present section of the work, then, is an attempt to set forth these rules in a clear and systematic manner.

India's
Hood Unveiled
𝔅𝔬𝔬𝔨 𝔗𝔴𝔬

CHAPTER I.

THE NATURE OF THE HUMAN MIND.

It was reserved for the closing of the 19th and the
opening of the 20th century to have revealed to it the
newer interpretations of the God-Nature of man. The
relation of man's mind to the God-mind has been established. The faculties of his individual mind have been
demonstrated and understood.

Mind is Master. What you train your mind to think,
your body— which is its servant—will show forth into
visibility, for mind and body is one and the same substance.

THE DUAL MIND.—The human mind consists of two
distinct parts, *viz., the conscious and the sub-conscious
mind.* Sometimes they are distinguished as the *objective* and the *subjective* mind. It is by means of the

conscious and *subconscious* faculties of your individual mind, and the proper training of the same, that you are to recreate your body and its environments that it will the more nearly conform to your desired condition and state.

The conscious and sub-conscious mind stand in exactly the same relation to each other as the mind and body. The consciousness directs the sub-consciousness what it shall believe and do. The sub-consciousness immediately proceeds to show forth in action, the directions or suggestion given to, never stopping to question as to the truth or falsity of these suggestions or whether they are for the best or not. This discrimination it leaves entirely to the conscious faculty.

The *conscious or objective* mind is the logical, "wide-awake" side of psychic life. Everything that is presented to the objective mind is argued with, reasoned out and the final result is carefully packed off into the pigeon-holes of the subjective mind. With the *objective* mind we are more or less familiar. It is what we ordinarily use in our every-day life. It is with the objective mind that you read these lines.

But the phase of consciousness denominated *subconscious or subjective* will be more obscure to the ordinary reader. It is with this that we have to deal more hereafter. It is that side of our consciousness which is amenable to *"suggestion"* and which lies in the background when we are "all there," but which is active during "reverie" when the imagination is awakened, and whenever the feats of somnambulism, hypnotism, mediumship, etc., are experienced.

The subjective mind can be influenced to almost any extent by "suggestion" and since it controls the functions, sensations and conditions of the body, we can easily understand how it is that curative treatment by means of will power is proved to be so effective.

It will be quite necessary for me to dwell further upon the *"subjective"* mind or to explain at greater length its *rationale and function.* Suffice it to say that all the experiments which we are able to make in the way of hypnotism, clairvoyance, trance, automatic writing, thought transference, etc., take place through its intervention, and that by means of it, most—if not all—of the hitherto "unexplained" phenomena of consciousness are rendered possible. Indeed, to perform the above experiments, all that the hypnotist does is to subdue the objective mind and give complete rest to it, while he wakes up the subjective mind, gives it the ascendancy and directs it by his *positive suggestions*.

At this point of the problem it will be well to discontinue further discussion, as the aim of this work is to be practical, rather than theoretical merely.

THE HINDU HYPNOGRAPH.

We have already learnt somewhat of the constitution of the mind; that it comprises two distinct phases of consciousness, and the functions of these respectively.

Now, all the phenomena presented under the "New Thought Science," it will be seen, is a function of the *subjective* mind, and it now remains for us to consider the means whereby such results as we are enabled to derive from the exercise of this mental factor are accomplished.

Those who have studied "Man" from the subjective standpoint and whose praiseworthy researches have entitled their opinions to respectful consideration, if not absolute credence, maintain that the realm of nature which we have denominated *subjective* is in reality a world quite as truly as the one of which we are ordinarily cognizant, and that we as, if not more, truly "live" in this department of the universe as we do in the physical.

HYPNOGRAPH. ITS PRINCIPLE.—It is a well-known physiological fact that, when the eye is fixed on any particular spot as on the hypnograph, *the objective mind* tends to stop its many and varied activities and

the *subjective mind* can be influenced to any great
extent by *suggestion*. Therefore, it is evident that, at
this moment, the *objective mind,* acting as an hypnotist
for the time being, can develop the *subjective mind,*
your real self, in any one particular direction, and
mould it to any shape. So most of the qualities that
go to constitute a successful hypnotist can be cultivated
in this manner. Amongst these may be mentioned
strength of will-power, concentration, health, self-confidence, fearlessness, courage, intelligence, benevolence,
perseverance, etc., etc.

DIRECTIONS.—Once you will be agreed, and determined to treat the matter seriously, select a calm and
quiet place in your private apartment. See that you
are absolutely alone and unobserved. The best time for
the experiment is in the morning, when the brain is
rested, the mind clear and refreshed and all the energies
alive and wide-awake. Seat yourself in a comfortable
position as on an easy chair or prop yourself up with
pillows on your bed. Sit quietly and relax all muscles
until they are free from *nervous tension*. Take the
"*hypnograph*" and hold it at a convenient and easy distance (say from 8" to 15") from your eyes; resign
yourself; think of nothing; make your mind as far as
possible a complete blank. Do not distract your mind
to examine any of the effects you will experience.
Breathe slowly, deliberately and calmly.

Keep your eyes steadily fixed on the *central white
spot of the hypnograph. Never stir your eyes from the
spot throughout the experiment.*

Now take up any one of the qualities you may choose,
say, "*Health.*" Commence your suggestions thus: "I
am perfectly healthy and will always continue to be so.
I can never get sickness of any sort. No. No headache, no fever, nothing of that sort can approach me.
I am very healthy. I am proof against every kind of
sickness. I am every moment getting stronger and
healthy by natural forces. I am enjoying absolute

health. I have a super-abundance of healthy, vital fluid in me that will ward off all sickness. I will always be healthy." Of course, I need hardly say that it is not necessary to confine yourself to keep to these words only. You may frame for yourself similar suggestions; but always let them be directed towards the same single *quality* chosen.

Take only one subject for each sitting and make the suggestions always *positive and decided*. Throughout the process keep your eyes steadily fixed on the white spot and avoid winking as far as possible; continue the *sitting* for about 15 or 20 minutes and keep up your suggestions throughout. If convenient, take 2 sittings a day. It is a good plan to commence your sittings at the same hour of the day always. The same subject will be taken for 4 or 5 sittings or more, till you are thoroughly satisfied that you have made enough progress with it. Any other subject, such as *courage*, may be treated similarly with suitable suggestions of your own.

On gazing at the spot for a few minutes or so, you may notice a sort of electric light or glory all round the black circle and along the rays which will be much attractive and will assist you in gazing steadily without winking. Sometimes the experiment may end in sleep or self-hypnotism. So much the better for you and your mind will be better developed. To meet such contingencies it is advisable for you to make very strong suggestions at the outset as to the duration of your sleep.

The foregoing method of self-culture has numerous advantages, it should be carried out in secret, never spoken about; but the fulness of life, thought and power attained should be diligently put into practical use in home-life and in contact with one's fellows. These processes rightly understood and practiced, demonstrate what the spirit of " I can" and "I will" can do for one in daily life. They lie at the foundation of successful hypnotic practice also.

SECRETS REVEALED.

The following instruments are indispensable to the successful hypnotist, and unless the student thoroughly masters them, he cannot make any progress in "New Thought Research." These are:

(1) *Health.* (2) *A Steady Will Power, Self-confidence and Concentration.* (3) *The Gaze.* (4) *The Pass.* (5) *Breathing.* (6) *Suggestion.*

HEALTH.—Whatever contributes to the health, vitality, goodness of heart and soundness of head of the hypnotist contributes to his hypnotic power. Health and vitality being the leading requisites, the health habits of the hypnotist should be good, his *will* strong, while patience, endurance, perseverance and sympathies should be marked features in his character. He should have a good, full, clear eye—colour not so much a matter of importance although persons of dark and hazel eyes make most successful experimenters and entertainers, and those of dark-blue, blue and violet eyes, successful healers.

Health is largely a question of constitution—it is in-bred—"Comes by Nature." Its maintenance is requisiste, but the *how* of its preservation and maintenance need not be entered upon here. Every hypnotist's life should be governed by "temperance in all things;" he should abstain from gross foods, impure drinks and associations, cultivate the good and true within himself. I might say that early and regular habits—morning bath, simple diet, adequate physical exercise, calmness and evenness of mind, will largely contribute to successful results. As for the rest, the New Thought adept is referred back to the hypnograph and works on simple hygienic rules.

THE WILL.—Next to health comes self-government, the development of *will* and the power to concentrate your energies. *Will* can be cultivated to a certain extent, as by the hypnograph, but the initial power of *will* will depend upon the phrenological development. A person deficient in Firmness, Self-esteem, Conscientiousness and Continuity is not likely to have a strong will. But if, in addition to the foregoing, they have those faculties which tend to timidity, lack of concentration, want of courage, as far as *will* is concerned, they would not make hypnotists at all. They are recommended again to the *hypnograph* as their last resource, and those that possess naturally a good *will* will fortify it by means of this wonderful instrument.

THE GAZE.—The other requisites, *viz., the gaze, the pass, breathing and suggestion,* can be easily cultivated. It must be remembered that these are not only the phantomimic language of the *will,* but that they are *vehicles* to convey *something* (human electricity or animal magnetism) from the operator to the subject. At least let the hypnotist act as if such were the case.

A steady *gaze* is essential. No one can hope to be master of "New Thought" if he cannot look another man or woman straight in the face. *The hypnograph* is the best means to cultivate the *gaze.* Its method of use has already been dealt with.

Again, in conversation, looking at a person (spoken to) quietly and steadily is a good plan also; don't stare, but look straight into his eyes. *Think* your thoughts as well as *speak* them. Never look at anything or anybody stupidly without having some dominant thought or idea working in your brain. There is not anything which will disconcert a courteous or discourteous liar than a *steady look.* In hypnotism you look with a purpose— your looks are to convey your intention and will. The wandering eye,—the blinking, winking or irresolute eye —never accomplished much good in this world hypnotically or any other way. When looking with a steady and quiet gaze, *think,* picture to your mind a scene, incident, phrase or a sentence. Should the person looked at give expression to the idea or words induced by you, repeat the process again and again as opportunity is afforded, until you have eliminated the elements of accident and coincident.

While there is some elements of thought transference connected with this, you must first gain the power of looking naturally and steadily at a person or an object for a considerable length of time without weariness. Make good use of the *Hypnograph*. Again, in taking exercise, or if out for a long walk, take in some *object* at a distance; while walking towards it, *gaze* steadily at it, as long as you can, without impairing vision, causing weariness to the eyes, winking, or tears to flow as in weeping.

The habit of steady gazing can be cultivated in many ways. The most trying is to look at a bright light—a jet of gas or lime light—for a certain period and in such a way as to cultivate the physical assurance of unweariness or inferiority when looking at a human being. Any sign of weakness, such as inability to look at a person about to be hypnotised steadily and for a length of time, would be prejudicial to successful results. The eyes should indicate strength of purpose and show no sign of weakness. For this the optic nerve and the muscles of the eyes and eyelids must be educated for their work.

Having gone so far in the cultivation of the gaze, commence to use it for some purpose. If at a place of amusement or at a lecture, sitting behind someone, look steadily at the nape of the neck with the *intention* of giving it a desire to turn round. This can be done by persevering practice—a small percentage of success will soon show you what can be done. You will begin to realise that the conscious direction of will by the eye becomes a most subtle and powerful mode or vehicle of thought.

The hypnotist must be powerful and his subjects very sensitive, receptive and well educated before the operations of the *will* wholly and solely are to be depended upon. It is not only right to cultivate the *will*, but the means whereby it may be best expressed or conveyed.

THE PASS.—The student of New Thought should be able to make all necessary movements with ease and grace—"natural like." I have seen some good souls possessing a fair aptitude for the science so awkward in their movements as to arouse the risible in their subjects. Nothing so keenly arouses the mind to resistance as the sense of the ludicrous on the one hand, or anger or empty scepticism on the other. All *passes* should be made quietly, easily and gracefully, and in some respects, with all the naturalness and kindliness with which a mother would pet a babe or a good nurse soothe the pains of a sick person. At the same time, *all passes* should be made *with purpose*—not with great physical, but always with great mental action.

VARIOUS KINDS OF PASSES.—Passes are made *long or general* and *short or local*. The long passes are from head to feet; and the short ones are directed to some particular region of the body. They are also made *"at distance"* or *"in contact,"* whether local or general in character. The manipulation with contact is of two kinds; it is accompanied either with considerable pressure or with light touching—manipulation with *strong* or with *light* contact.

HOW TO CULTIVATE THE "PASS."—The passes should be practiced so that they can be performed from half an hour to an hour and even longer, without apparently any physical weakness. A good plan for exercise might be adopted as follows:

Place a chair in the centre of a room (lock the door and proceed unobserved to work). Imagine a person seated on the chair, and take your stand opposite it for the purpose of putting him to sleep. Commence by making long passes at distance. The hands, with fingers extended and directed towards the eyes of the supposed subject should then be lowered gradually and naturally down to his feet—that is making the downward or magnetic pass. The hands have now to be raised so as to resume their original position. They should not be

raised up in front of the subject's body, but on each
side of him. The downward pass is to soothe or produce sleep; the upward pass, as above described, is to
enable you to repeat frequently the downward pass without undoing its work. In actual practice, mind-energy
or its concentration and *desired expression* is put into
your *downward pass.* No intention or concentration
of mind is put into the upward pass; at the same time
it is desirable to keep it clear of the body to prevent
that disturbance which accidental reverse passes sometimes make.

*Downward passes soothe or contribute to sleep; up-
ward passes to wakefulness. Upward passes with or
without intention never produce sleep.*

Local passes and "in contact" belong more particularly to the curative branch of the subject, and are used
more frequently when there is no intention to produce
sleep, but to cure disease. Of course short passes can
be and are made locally without contact for the same
purpose. Sleep is often produced by local passes con-
fined to the head, chest, arms and sometimes terminating at the hypochondrium or pit of the stomach.

BREATHING.—Certain wise physicians cured diseases
by "blowing" or breathing. Now, there is an art in
breathing. It can be cultivated. The method I suggest, like all my methods, is natural and healthy—of
great benefit to the individual even though he never influenced anyone electrically.

Each morning on rising, and at the earliest period of
the day when fresh air can be obtained, the New
Thought adept should stand erect, with chest well
thrown out, mouth shut and *inhale slowly* through the
nostrils and *fully expand his lungs.* It may be several
weeks before he can take good long breaths and retain
them, say, one or two minutes in the lungs before exhaling. He should not exhale rapidly—on the contrary, he should exercise as much control over the last
act as on the former two, namely, the inspiration of the

air and the power of retaining it in the lungs. To start with, each of the three operations may be exercised to the length of 10 seconds, gradually extending the period until each can be kept up for one minute.

Having so far acquired power in this direction, the next step is to know how to use it. Breathing can be used in several ways. Hot breathing or air expired from the chest is soothing, healing, curative. Cold breathing or air blown slowly and deliberately from the compressed lips has most salutary effects and is arousing and wakeful in character. Some remarkable effects are obtained by breathing through flannel or clothing.

There is yet another kind of breathing, to which the name *"Kill-Fear Secret"* has been very aptly applied.

THE KILL-FEAR SECRET.—Stand erect in military position. *"Attention."* Head up, chin in, chest elevated, shoulders thrown back and down. Exhaust the dead air as completely as possible from the lungs. Close one of the nostrils by pressure of your hand, and through the other nostril *inhale air suddenly* into your lungs, filling the abdominal cavity so that *only the lower portion of the lungs are distended to the fullest possible extent.* A distinct pressure must be felt at the diaphragm or the lower part of your abdomen during the process. The upper chest need not be extended.

Then *exhale rapidly* through the nostril that was kept closed until now.

Time taken as follows: Inhaling—½ a second, retention—2 seconds, exhaling—½ a second. In all 3 secs. Repeat this operation 5 or 6 times in quick succession.

USES.—Success in varying degrees is immediate. Results are sure, and the effect is an astonishing mental or rather emotional calmness. This means you have discovered the secret of emotional control. You can force all acute mental distress of an emotional nature to leave you instantly. You are absolute master of yourself henceforth. The nerve currents and the blood circulation in the *solar plexus* or emotional brain have been stimulated into a normal condition. Don't overdo this exercise through your elation over the discovery. Use it only when you feel you need it and can stand it.

Among the emotions which can be controlled by this method are: Acute worry, fear, anxiety, anger, grief, passion, stage-fright and nervous excitement.

The cultivation of the steady eye, the graceful pass, and the long and powerful breath develop the health the physical and mental powers. They help to strengthen and concentrate the will. The mesomeric or hypnotic influence is only valuable as it proceeds from a sound body and is directed by a sound mind. The foregoing simple processes are directed mainly to achieve that end.

CHAPTER II.

SUGGESTION.

What is suggestion in Mental Science? Suggestion means *any impression, physical or mental,* through touch, sound, words, writing or direction to think or to do, *which the subject can appreciate in a suggestible state or hypnosis;* and hypnosis is a state more or less allied to sleep and its border-lands; *its essential characteristic is not sleep but an induced state of susceptibility or receptivity of suggestion.*

Bernheim says: "I take care to say that sleep is not essential; that the hypnotic influence, whence comes the benefit, may exist without sleep, and that many patients are hypnotised, although they do not sleep. If the patient does not shut his eyes or keep them shut, I do not require them to be fixed on mine or my fingers for any length of time; for it sometimes happens that they remain wide open indefinitely, and instead of the idea of sleep being conceived, only a rigid fixation of the eyes results; in this case, closing of the eyelids by the operator succeeds better. * * *

"Passes or gazing at the eyes or fingers of the operator are only useful in concentrating the attention, and are not absolutely essential." To arouse, arrest and concentrate the attention is the main object in the induction of hypnosis—not sleep. Hypnotism, defined by Bernheim, means "the induction of a peculiar physical condition which increases the *susceptibility to suggestion;* but it is not the necessary preliminary; *it is suggestion that rules hypnotism.*"

(93)

Perhaps at this stage the student may not be able to realize many of the points referred to above. He will be better able to appreciate them when he comes to the practice of human magnetism, which will be dealt with at great length in later chapters. But the foregoing is mentioned to bring into view the importance of *suggestion in New Thought*. It is the governing and directing cause of all experimental and therapeutic effects. The reader, ere he commences practice in these lines, has now two things to keep in view:

1. Either the suggestible state is natural, or it can be induced; if necessary, his first object will be to induce that state.

2. That state of receptivity being there, or induced, the current of the subject's thoughts is to be directed and strengthened by *suggestion*.

Having given suggestion, properly, to a subject in a suggestible condition, such suggestion cannot, or rather will not, be resisted. To give suggestions properly is, in the main, a matter of experience, confidence, ability, in which the intelligence (character, health) of the operator is an important factor.

The next and most natural factor is the character (intelligence and disposition) of the *subject* whose *concentrated attention* is to be aroused, educated by hypnotic processes and directed, in the first place, to some simple object with a view to modify ordinary intellectual activity and induce a receptive state.

The most important stage is the beginning stage, viz., the induction of the foregoing state. The rest is comparatively easy, and becomes more and more so as the hypnotist and the subject enter into a better knowledge of each other's ways—harmony or *rapport*. Another point to be considered. *Suggestions* have to be repeated in order to make a groove of their own in the mental structure of the subject. Drops of water wear away a stone; repeated suggestions wear away resistance and are finally accepted or appreciated by the subject. In ordinary education we appreciate the value of *At-*

tention and Repetition in fixing a sentence, lesson or idea in the mind. Even time is necessary to fix an impression, as all who have made a study of the phenomena of memory will duly appreciate. A sentence must be repeated over and over again to deepen and fix the impressions so that it will make its own special groove in the physical organs of the mind.

Attention and Repetition are the key-notes of successful suggestion. The attention of the subject must be aroused and kept, while repetition helps to fix the *new idea—the change of direction to the current of one's thoughts which the repeated suggestions seek to establish.*

The value and importance of several sittings and repeated suggestions will be more fully understood when we realize that the majority of persons suffering from disease, as well as the greater number who suffer from bodily complaints in consequence of wrong thinking and morbid fears have been and are constantly giving themselves *false suggestions.* They are affected by the vile literature of unblushing quacks, who care nothing about, and know less of, therapeutics; whose only object is to frighten people and line their own pockets. *Morbid Fears of Contagion or Infection*—selfish fears in a thousand phases—help to make them all and keep them so.

Persons knowing that one or other of their grandparents or parents have died from pneumonia, consumption, cancer, heart disease, kidney trouble, apoplexy or some other complaint—perhaps there has also been some form of mental disease or marked peculiarity of manner in one or other of their progenitors; it matters little what, but it is sufficient to know that these things have been; they dwell upon history, retail the facts to friends, express fear for themselves and say, "You know his father (or so and so on his father's side) died of——; I am afraid of——; he has such and such symptoms;" or these people themselves get into their head that they are likely to get ill and die of one or other of the foregoing diseases, because it is in the family, until every feeling is distorted to fit in with the special trouble which is believed to be hereditary and must be theirs. These *false suggestions*, based on morbid fears do evil work.

All these erroneous suggestions as well as fixed ideas of an undesirable character have to be uprooted by counter-suggestions to give a change—a healthy change of direction to the mind. These new, correct and sympathetic suggestions will have double force:

(1) From the mind, intelligence, experience, personality or hypnotic influence of the operator; and

(2) From the suggestibility of the patient whose attention has been successfully concentrated upon some non-exciting and acceptable object or notion.

Then the healing or therapeutic suggestions are repeated and repeated, mentally rubbed in so as to deepen and fix them, giving a new and correct direction to the thought forces of the patient.

All diseases curable by medicines are curable by *suggestion;* brain and nervous diseases are more easily curable by *suggestion* than by any other means. Neuralgias, whether in the head or face or eleswhere in the body; rheumatism in various stages, various forms of headaches, whether arising from conditions within the brain or as reflexes from the body; neurasthenia—including the foregoing—hysteria, insomnia, hypochondriases, mental and moral perversions, dipsomania, drug and allied perversities, evil habits from nail-biting to positively demoralising and incorrigible weakness, theft and indecencies; excessive nervousness, sensitiveness, stammering, lack of moral fibre, strength of will, etc.; forgetfulness, despondency, dyspepsia, constipation, self-consciousness, bashfulness, morbid fears of lightning, thunder, people, places, examinations and stage-fright, and more serious troubles, *i. e.,* nervous deafness, blindness, paralysis, epilepsy, and in many cases insanity.

In many chronic and even functional diseases *suggestion* has proved an effective cure, when found intractable to medicinal treatment.   It will therefore be found that *suggestion*—while not a cure-all—will cure diseases amenable to medicinal substances, *and others which have not been amenable, and indeed cannot be cured by the practice of medicine.*

This is the great value of *suggestion in Hypnotism.*

This section of the work (Part I) embraces the whole machinery of "New Thought Science" in any of its phases; the principles dealt with here should therefore be thoroughly studied and applied before the student can successfully step into the Practical Plane.

CHAPTER III.

HYPNOTISM.

"Animal magnetism" or "Electrical Psychology" is the name used to describe the subtle sympathetic life-force by which certain persons are able to influence, attract and even cure other persons. If their influence is good, they are said to impart a *"healthy magnetism."* Mesmerism is a term of similar import, and was given to the practice of *human magnetism* by the followers of Mesmer, just as the electrical fluid was called galvanism after Galvani. Hypnotism is a more modern term, originally suggested and employed by Dr. Braid, Manchester, and for all practical purposes is synonymous to the foregoing:

There are, however, shades of difference between the "theory of suggestion or Hypnotism" and the "theory of Mesmerism or animal magnetism" and between their respective modes of procedure. A separate chapter will therefore be devoted to "Mesmerism," so that the student will be able to better differentiate their uses and practical applications.

NATURE OF HYPNOTISM.—Hypnotism means the theory and practical manipulation of the phenomena of *hypnosis*. Now, *hypnosis* is usually described as artificially induced sleep or a trance-like condition of mind and body. But though this is the definition generally adopted, yet it leaves aside, as I think, the chief characteristic of the phenomenon, *hypnosis*, as distinct from ordinary sleep, and which gives it its special interest. I mean

(98)

the *rapport* established thereby between the hypnotised subject and the hypnotiser, which makes the former susceptible of receiving suggestions of the latter, or, even, so disconnects the hypnotised subject from all other objects save the hypnotiser as to bring the former more or less completely under the control of the latter.

"The hypnotic sleep," Braid informs us, "is the very antithesis of opposite mental and physical condition to that which precedes and accompanies *common sleep;* for the latter arises from a diffused state of mind, or complete loss of power of fixing the attention, with suspension of voluntary power. * * * The state of mental concentration, however, which is the basis of *hypnotic* sleep, enables the subject to exhibit various passive or active manifestations, such as insensibility rigidity and entire prostration or inordinate energy of physical power, according to the train of ideas and motives which may arise spontaneously in his mind, or be addressed to it by others through impressions on his physical organs."

This is Braid's view. It is certainly one view out of many which appears correct, according to the aspect from which we distinguish hypnotic from ordinary sleep; although the latter can be converted into the former, just as ordinary sleep verges into somnambulism, through certain mental impressions received in the preceding waking states, or arising from pathological conditions in associations.

One point to be noted; "the audible suggestions and sensible impressions addressed to the sleeper, if not intense enough to awaken entirely, seldom do more than excite a dream, in which ideas pass through his mind without causing definite physical acts; but, on the other hand, the active and concentrated state of mind engendered by the process for producing *nervous sleep* are carried *into* the sleep, and in many instances, excite the sleeper without awaking, to speak or exhibit physical manifestations of the suggestions received through words audibly uttered in his hearing, or ideas previously existing in his mind, or excited by touches or passes of the operator, which direct the attention of the sleeper to different parts, or excite into action certain combinat'ons of muscles and thereby direct his current of thought."

In the foregoing, we have a simple outline of hypnotism as it appeared to Braid; and giving it a modern application, it will be seen:—

1.   That hypnosis is a state of sleep induced, and in this state a more or less effective condition of passive receptivity, susceptibility or suggestibility obtains.

2.   That the *modus operandi* of inducing hypnosis and the ideas associated therewith pass into that state when induced, and are intensified or modified by the hypnotist, as he may deem most desirable, and within the limitation of the subject's approval.

3.   That the subject responds to the ideas or trains of thought, arising spontaneously in his own mind, to audible suggestions and impressions—physical—made by touches on his body or by passes over it and through these, *his mind is led to concentrate on the object most desired.*

The practical hypnotist first seeks—with the conscious co-operation of the patient or subject—to bring about a state of hypnosis, passivity and suggestibility, and then by verbal suggestions—with or without contact—to arouse and confirm certain trains of thought in the patient, in order to bring about the *end sought,* i. e., to direct the current of his thought on *the lines of the least resistance.*

WHO CAN BE HYPNOTIZED?—Hypnosis is a state of susceptibility normal to, and possessed by, more or less, all individuals.   Prof. James Coates, Ph. D., F. A. S., in his "Practical Hypnotist," p. II, says:—

"Discarding the idea of only certain percentages of the people being susceptible to hypnotism, I have myself long since arrived at the conclusion that *all persons can be hypnotised*—that is, if the necessary conditions and precautions are taken—those living in warmer

climes furnishing the greatest percentage of spontaneously affected, while at home (England) several sittings
may be necessary to educate the patient into the suggestible state, hypnosis and its approximate states (for
many persons become suggestible who are neither drowsy
nor become sleepy) as generally understood. Then,
again, the age of the patient has a relation to states of
susceptibility. Liebault hypnotised 92 per cent, of his
patients, and Bernheim expressed the opinion that physicians who cannot at least hypnotise 80 per cent. of
hospital patients have no right to express an opinion
of the subject of hypnotism, while Wettersbrand (Swe-
den), Van Reuterghem (Amsterdam), Van Eden, too,
as well as Liebault, in France, substantiate the conclusion that the majority of patients, be they French, Dutch
or Swedish—the latter, at least, are neither excitable,
hysterical nor easily impressed—are equally hypnotis-
able. Coming to the relation of age to susceptibility—
all persons under 14 can be hypnotised—the percentages of exceptions, according to Prof. Beaunis,
vary with age. From 14 to 21, 10.3 per cent.; 21
to 28, 9.1 per cent.; 28 to 35, 5.9 per cent.; 35 to 42,
8 2 per cent.; 49 to 56, 4.4 per cent.; 56 to 63, 14.4 per
cent; above 63, 13.5 per cent. of failures. This is based
on practice with French subjects, and on the induction
of a *state of hypnosis,* and is so far interesting. But as
a matter of fact, patients who cannot be affected by one
hypnotist can be affected by another—showing that the
ability, experience and influence of the individual operator is a factor, although not the sole factor, in the induction of hypnosis."

It is generally believed that only weak-minded, soft
and hysterical persons can be successfully hypnotised—
that persons of robust health, will and character cannot
be so affected. There never was a greater mistake.
Reichenbach for many years selected his sensitives from
delicate and hysterical persons while pursuing investigations into odylic force. He, however, soon discovered
his error, and found that healthy men and women made

the best sensitives for his investigations. Dr. Braid fell into the same error.

Charcot and others, including the whole range of recent hypnotists, have revived this error. The experience of all hypnotists—past and present—worthy of the name is this: *the healthier and finer the organization the more perfect and exalted the manifestations.*

There are relative conditions of superiority and inferiority in hypnotists and sensitives only. I have hypnotised men who were my superiors in every way—health, strength of body and mind—the only conditions of difference consisting of this important fact, *that for the time being they approached the subject with open minds—a desire to get at truth—and sat down with a non-resistant attitude of mind and perfectly willing to be hypnotised.*

In the majority of cases the 7th or 8th *sitting* suffices to overcome all difficulties, and induce sleep in the most healthy and vigourous. There have, however, been exceptions to this.

Don't waste time with a man who makes a bet through pride, vanity or ignorance, that he can't be hypnotised. Don't waste health and energy trying to influence him just then. His manner and words indicate that he will arouse all his faculties to resist you, presenting thereby positive and antagonistic mental conditions for you to overcome. Men have done this. If you really want to hypnotise them, the best plan is to throw them off their guard as to your intentions. But as soon as their opposition has cooled down a little, proceed gently and *steadily to impress them* with what hypnotism has done and can do; thus gradually and surely psychologise them, leading up to, and preparing them for, the final *coup*. In the end it may not be so difficult to hypnotise them as they at first imagined. The persistent man of business, the advocate of certain views—temperance, anti-slavery or what not—the man with "a mission" the doctor of medicine, preacher and lover, all adopt this method more or less unconsciously, because naturally;

the hypnotist, detecting the law, applies it consciously—
that is all.

DIFFERENT STAGES IN HYPNOTISM.—The phenomena
presented by persons under the influence of hypnotism
are various, as well as the methods by which the effects
are produced. The former are classed under four degrees, as follows. The latter will be presented under
"Modes of Procedure."

1. *The Waking Stage.*—Here the subject is under
partial control, the intellect and senses retaining, apparently, their usual powers and susceptibility. The
experiments in this stage are exceedingly interesting to
all concerned, especially in case of a drawing room or
other entertainment. These are useful preliminaries to
the induction of *hypnosis-proper*.

2. *The Cataleptic Stage.*—When the subject reaches
this stage, the hypnotic sleep or *coma* is complete. The
senses refuse to perform their respective functions. The
subject is therefore unconscious to pain. He possesses
no volition, does not respond to mental or verbal suggestions—nervous muscular excitability appears to be
absent—and in whatever position the various parts of
the body are placed, they will remain in that po ition.

3. *The Lethargic Stage.*—Here the subject is a helpless lump of inanity; the muscles are unflexed, flaccid
and flabby, the body is in all respects like that condi-
tioned by a dead faint, or in a lesser degree, by the
coma of drunkenness. Surgical operations can be performed in either stage, without real or apparent pain to
the subject.

4. *The Somnambulistic Stage.*—In this stage the
subject wakes up within himself. The faculties become
responsive to hypnotic influence, direction and suggestion, the sensitive becoming largely an irresponsible
agent, thinking, seeing and hearing only as permitted
or as directed by the hypnotist. It is in this stage that
the phreno-hypnotic and mostly all other experiments
are conducted, whether deemed hypnotic or mesmeric.
With good subjects, memory, reflection and imagination

can be intensified and exalted, the past recalled by the present, and action done therein confessed, should such be determined upon by the operator. It is in this stage that the *rapport* of hypnosis is fully established between the hypnotist and his subject. The hypnotised subject can be made to experience the wildest illusions of sense and perform most absurd actions. Thus he can be easily persuaded that a glass of water is tea, wine or vinegar, or *vice versa*, and can be made to stroke an imaginary cat or shrink from an imaginary lion.

These four stages may be progressively developed on the same subject. The majority of hypnotic subjects pass from *the cataleptic to the somnambulistic stage* without any apparent intervening condition.

CHAPTER IV.

THE PRACTICAL HYPNOTIST.

A WORD OF PRECAUTION.—We now come to practice. Before entering into the operating room, let me again advise the beginner that he should not lightly enter upon the task, unless he has fully grasped the principles explained in previous chapters and is thorough with the practical application of the simple rules laid down in the concluding chapters of Part I. Many persons have foolishly commenced practice of hypnotism without fully knowing its principles—commenced to try experiments with no other knowledge than that of having seen some other person experiment. I quote here a notable instance of such folly, described by Prof. Coates in the following words:

"Some years ago I gave a series of demonstrations at the Queen's rooms, Bold street, Liverpool. A gentleman residing in Bootle was present with his family one evening. On returning home he thought, for the 'fun of the thing,' he would 'try his hand.' He had no doubt but he could do just as well as myself, as he afterwards told me. He succeeded in putting his footman asleep, and of getting him to do several things, which he (the gentleman), his family and servants enjoyed amazingly. He was in rapture with his more than expected success, the subject being exceedingly passive and docile in his hands. He, however, forgot how to de-mesmerise or wake the subject up. Becoming perplexed and excited, the poor footman followed suit. One person suggested

(105)

one thing, another, another thing. This gentleman tried to carry out the various suggestions, but the poor victim was fast retrograding from bad to worse. Smelling salts were applied to his nose and water thrown over him; these efforts only unduly excited him. He groaned and cried, and acted in a very strange manner. A messenger was sent into town; at considerable trouble I was found, and at 4 o'clock in the morning I arrived at his house. I saw how things stood and proceeded to de-mesmerise his footman by the following process: I got every person in the house who had touched the young man to take hands and join in a circle, the gentleman who had mesmerized the youth taking his (footman's) left hand, while I completed the circle by taking his right hand.

"I counselled passivity and calmness on all and explained to them the risk of indiscriminating experiments, and the dangers which might arise therefrom, and pointed out that this was a bad case of 'cross mesmerism.' By forming the circle I sought to tone down the tumult, calm the patient, and subject all to my influence. At the end of 15 minutes I broke up the circle, placed myself in dominant contact with the patient and de-mesmerised him. The lesson was not readily forgotten by either the gentleman or his servants. * * *"

In proceeding to work it is well to bear in mind the statement of Moll, one of the most successful medical hypnotists, "that any little inconvenience which hypnotism may at first cause, is not to be compared with the benefits it confers." The next thing is to avoid faulty methods, over-anxiety for results, and under all circumstances the operator should keep a level head. Nervous people may become, for a little while, more nervous—that is not due to hypnotism, but rather to fear and ignorance, and more or less "old wives' tales" by which they are affected or prejudiced.

The practitioner should not force results, cause a patient to stare too long at a bright object, or unduly stimulate any of the senses. He should not seek to force psychical development in the way of extraordinary play of psychic faculty, clairvoyance, clair-audiance, etc., and at the conclusion of each sitting all suggestions should be neutralised before waking the patient; and finally, care should be taken to see that the patient is agreeably and fully awakened to the normal state again.

These remarks apply especially to experimental investigations and practices. But the neutralisation of healing suggestions is not necessary, be they immediate or post-hypnotic. All that is required is to quietly, firmly and kindly awaken the patient. Should there be any little inconvenience felt by the patient, the operator will remove that.

We will now enter into the operating room and witness some of the most useful and most simple modes of procedure. In all cases there are three inevitable stages:

1. The induction of hypnosis.
2. Suggestions and experiments.
3. Awakening the subject.

Our attention will just now be given to the first of these. For the induction of hypnosis is the "Little go" and the *pons asinorum* of all beginners. In the present chapter we will deal with the preliminary or waking stage experiments, which are, so to say, the most important part of the process. It is these that educate the subject in his will-power and attention, and gradually, but certainly, lead up to hypnosis; at the same time, the experiments are, in their own way, interesting and thus relieve the beginner of much fatigue and further assist him in developing his own powers progressively. These experiments are suitably arranged below and it is advised not to proceed to the sleeping stage before all the experiments are successfully tried. Further, you should not attempt any of the waking experiments of a higher order before you are thoroughly successful with the preceding ones. You should be highly methodical and proceed in order with each subject.

WAKING EXPERIMENTS.—1. Devitalising any part of the body.

2. Falling backwards.
3. Falling forwards.
4. *Fastening the hands.*
5. Stiffening the elbow-joint.
6. Stiffening the knee-joint and making the subject unable to move about.
7. Making a cane or wand stick to any part of the body.
8. Making any light body very heavy, so that the subject is unable to carry it.
9. Striking the subject dumb.
10. *Closing his eyes.*

After these any experiment that you may devise can be performed. In fact, when you are successful with the 4th experiment you will find the others are comparatively easy. With any one particular subject, if you fail to perform any experiment (say the 6th), the *sitting* at once terminates and a second sitting is arranged the next day advantageously at about the same hour. Then the operations are commenced over again from the very first to the 6th experiment. If you don't succeed at this sitting also, try a third, fourth or even a fifth sitting till you thoroughly succeed. Then you may proceed to the 7th and other experiments.

Note.—This method is specially recommended for beginners. Of course, as the student advances in practice he may dispense with *these waking experiments* one after another or vary their order to suit his own taste and discretion; or he may commence experimenting after the manner of the next chapter.

MODES OF PROCEDURE.—Preliminary.—Make your subject feel at home, disabuse his mind of fear, doubt, anxiety and scepticism. Some trusted friend of the subject should also be present, especially if the subject happen to be a lady; while not absolutely necessary, it simplifies matters very much both for the operator and patient. Remove, if possible, all elements which are likely to arouse or excite the patient's mind.

To succeed, the subject must either be naturally sensitive to your *influence*—*i. e.*, passive and receptive—or, he must be made so. Everything you do must tend to that condition. By action and speech—in everything you must show you know fully what you are about; there must be no timidity, hesitancy or half-heartedness exhibited in your manner. You must create the instinctive feeling in the mind of your patient, "that is a man I can trust, that man or person will do me good," *and you will do it.*

1. DEVITALISING ANY PART OF THE BODY.—This is an experiment to be done by the *subject himself*. All that you do in this is to give him proper instructions and the subject must do it by the sheer exercise of his *will*. Consider the hand first. *Devitalising the hand means to take off all life from it at will.* Let your subject sit or stand erect; ask him to withdraw all voluntary action from it, so that in all respects it resembles a stick. Let him imagine that there is no joint at his shoulder. What should happen? The hand must obey the law of gravity and must fall down of its own accord. He ought not to force it down of his own accord, neither should he resist its tendency to fall. After a few trials he will be able to do it quite satisfactorily.

Or, you may proceed thus: Ask the subject to hold his right hand in a horizontal position and let it be supported at a little in front of the elbow joint by means of the fore-finger of his left hand which is held underneath in a vertical position. Ask him to put neither more nor less than the just weight of his right hand upon his forefinger; that is to say, let him not exert any voluntary force of the hand upon the finger, nor should he hold up the hand by means of the muscles of the upper arm so as to reduce the proper weight of the arm. There should be no voluntary action whatever. If the finger is now withdrawn suddenly, the hand must droop down. You will show this personally by devitalising your own hand, and you will see that the hand falls down with perfect freedom the moment the supporting finger is withdrawn. In like manner, the left hand, the leg, and, in fact, the whole body, can be devitalised at will. This is a very healthy exercise and must be practised by the subject with advantage. After you are satisfied that he is thorough with this exercise you may commence the second experiment somewhat as follows:

2. FALLING BACKWARDS.—Let your subject stand erect, place his heels together and drop his hands to his sides. Ask him to dismiss all thoughts from his mind and close his eyes. Let there be no *nervous tension* anywhere in his body. He should not exercise any force on his feet and his whole body must stand like a stick, perfectly devitalised and free to move about in any direction. You may just test this before you proceed further.

Stand behind him and place the palm of your left hand on his forehead and the tight fist of your right hand at the back of his head just above the nape of the neck; apply a slight pressure with both your hands (in this position) and keep his head erect; but don't apply any force with your hands that may tend to push him backwards. All the while his eyes are kept closed and you go on with your suggestions thus: "You are going to fall backwards, to fall backwards. Very shortly you will be falling backwards. Very soon an *influence* will come upon you that will push you backwards. Do not resist it, but give free play to it; on the other hand, do not fall of your own accord. You are about to fall backwards. The *influence* is on you now. You are going to fall. You *are* falling now, falling backwards you are falling, falling, falling backwards. I see you are falling backwards, etc., etc.," and so on gradually raising your voice (which should always be firm and gentle) as you get to the end; and slowly withdrawing your hands.

Or, you may proceed thus: Place your hands upon his shoulders for a few minutes. Then concentrate your *passes* down his spine to the small of his back These passes are made as if charging with your *in fluence*. Having done so several times, place the tips

of your fingers lightly upon the back, on the spine, level
with the lower part of the shoulder blades, and proceed
to make drawing passes with *the intention* of drawing
the person to you. Throughout the whole process continue your suggestions.

3. FALLING FORWARDS.—In this, as well as in the
previous experiment, assure your subject that there will
be no danger in falling and that you are ready by his
side to help him and see that he does not fall flat on the
floor. Stand in front of him and ask him to direct his
eyes to yours and keep them there. Tell him that
throughout the process he should maintain a steady
gaze, and as far as possible, without winking. You are,
of course, trained to purpose and would never wink at
all during the experiment. You must look steadily at
his organ of *individuality*, which is situated at the root
of the nose, just below the forehead and between the
eyes. Hold his head with gentle pressure by his temples with both your open hands, but never exercise by
means of your hands, any tendency to *pull* him forwards. Everything must be done by your *will, concentration, and suggestion.* Proceed in a manner similar
to the previous experiment, strongly *willing* and suggesting steadily and firmly that he should *fall forwards.*
Frame your own suggestions.

4. FASTENING THE HANDS.—As before, direct your
eyes to the subject's *organ of individuality* while he is
gazing at your eyes. Ask him to firmly and tightly in-
terlock the fingers of his hands and hold them up to
their fullest extent towards you and maintain a horizontal position. *Will* strongly that his hands become
fastened together so tight as to become inseparable, try
he ever so hard. Make a few *local passes with light
contact* on the hands, commencing from his wrist down-
wards; occasionally you may make a longer pass from
his shoulder down to the hands. From the commence-
ment of the experiment keep up the attention of the
subject and maintain his *concentration on fastening his*

hands by means of your *suggestions*, which must be quietly and firmly given, and may be in the following or similar terms:

"I am about to fasten your hands. In a short time, in a very few moments there will come a binding force on your hands. The *influence* is already there now, your hands are being fastened, the force is but slight at present; it is growing, your hands are becoming tighter, tighter still. Don't attempt to separate them now; but be passive and allow *my influence* to work its course. I will presently give you the word 'try,' when your hands will be completely fastened. You may try your utmost to separate them then. However hard you may try, you cannot possibly separate them. Your hands are becoming tighter now, tighter and tighter every moment. (Always keep your eyes on mine.) Your hands *are* tight now, *very tight*, tigher still; they are absolutely tight (gradually raise your voice and let it be firm and decisive); you won't be able to separate them. Your hands are very, very tight. It is impossible to separate them now, utterly impossible. I am going to give you the word 'try.' You cannot possibly separate your hands; they are, as it were, rivetted together. Now, *'try!' try with all your might;* you cannot separate; it is thoroughly impossible; possibly you may break your hands in the attempt. You cannot separate your fingers.   *   *   *"

Finally, make a few counter passes and say firmly, "Your hands have resumed their normal condition. They can be separated now."

I cannot impress this too strongly upon you that this experiment is, as it were, the stumbling-block of all beginners. You should exercise great care in will, concentration, gaze and passes, all simultaneously. But never be disheartened by failures. If you fail once, call for a next sitting, and a next, and try again. When you succeed in this experiment, you may rest assured that all the succeeding experiments are at your fingers' ends.

The method of procedure in the following experiments is very similar to the present one and you can apply suitable suggestions in each case. In this connection I should strongly recommend beginners to witness as many entertainments as may come under their notice. The *passes* in each case are *local* in character and in *light contact*.

CHAPTER V.

HOW TO INDUCE HYPNOTIC SLEEP.

RELATIVE POSITION OF SUBJECT AND HYPNOTIST.—
The subject is invited to take his seat on an easy chair
or asked to lie on a sofa (with his back to the light,
which should shine on your face). He is further invited to make himself comfortable, think of nothing in
particular, not to be over-anxious, and simply—as far
as lies in his power—follow the directions given. If the
subject be on a chair, you can stand conveniently in
front of or at the right side of your subject. Should he
be lying on a couch, you may draw in a chair; and in all
cases your position should be that which will make the
subject slightly raise his eyes to see you. His muscles
should be relaxed, all limbs flexed, hands and arms comfortably bestowed; but you are just the opposite; your
muscles are braced and you are correspondingly positive,
alert and self-confident, as the subject is, or ought to
be, negative and receptive.

Next for 3 minutes or so, take hold of his left hand
in an easy, comfortable manner by your right hand.
The best position is to put the ball of your thumb on
his, while your thumb itself crossing his wrist applies
a gentle pressure on the nerves just above the wrist.
Place your left hand on his head for a couple of minutes, covering his forehead at the right temple with
the hollow of your hand, with fingers resting on head
and your thumb converging towards *"Individuality."*
Your eyes are, of course, directed to his *organ of indi-*

(114)

viduality throughout. Exercise your *will* calmly and steadfastly towards the desired end—*sleep.* This is *taking the contact.*

The next step is to quietly arouse the subject's attention and keep it. Suppose the subject is in a chair, you will take your stand erect within easy distance at one side or in front of him, and speak in a quiet, kind, but firm and decisive voice, suggesting both assurance and comfort. You may either ask your subject to direct his eyes to yours or you may hold the fore-finger of your right hand from with 5″ or 6″ of the subject's eyes and slightly above them and ask him to look steadily at the tip of your finger; or you may substitute a button or the tip of your wand for the same purpose; in a short time he will experience the hypnotic influence. Inform him, if he feels any strange or peculiar feelings —a sinking sensation, darkness of vision, nervous tremulousness, drowsiness, or an inclination to sleep, not to resist, but *give way.* It will be alright and you will see him through.

While this talk is quietly and amiably going on, the subject continues looking at these non-excitable objects. In a quieter tone commence your "sleep talk," and as you go along, your tone will become more and more muffled and monotonous. "You are getting restful and easy, drowsy, very sleepy, drowsy and inclined to sleep. You are restful and drowsy, sleepy, restful and easy," slowly several times.

"You are very drowsy and your eyes are becoming heavier and heavier. They will close of their own accord very soon. Your sight is getting dim; the eyelids are very heavy. You are feeling sleepy, s-l-e-e-p-y. You cannot keep your eyes open long; you are sleepy, sleepy, sleepy; you are feeling sleepy, sleepy, sleepy, s-l-e-e-p-y," several times with slight alterations.

"You are sleeping, sleeping, sleeping, soundly sleeping; nothing can disturb your sleep; you are soundly sleeping, nothing can disturb you. Sleep on. Sleep soundly. That is it. You are sleeping, sleeping sleeping soundly; soundly sleeping; nothing can disturb you. No noise in the world can disturb your sleep. Sleep on. Sleep soundly. You are sleeping, sound asleep; fast asleep you are. No earthly voice can wake you from this excellent sleep other than mine; *fast asleep, asleep, sound asleep; you are sleeping soundly, fast asleep, sound asleep,*" several times, the latter more decisively but not louder.

All the while, you maintain your fixed position and steady gaze; but throughout there should be neither vulgar staring nor thumb-pressure.

Meantime, the eyelids have dropped, trembled and closed. A slight alteration in the breathing has taken place or other sleep symptoms have shown themselves.

You may withdraw your hands now, but not your eyes and commence your *passes* along with your suggestions. The tone of your voice is now to be slightly raised and the last sentence slightly altered and repeated, and the subject passes into a slight doze or into a deeper stage. [The former is quite sufficient in the majority of cases for curative purposes.] By means of *the passes* you further *charge* the brain with *your influence,* always downward over the head and face—forehead, top-head, side head and back-head—all coming under your direction, so far as such passes can be made with *direct intent* and with ease and comfort; at the same time raise your voice and repeat the sleep suggestions, while making the passes gently and soothingly over the face and form of the subject, and assuring him "you are fast asleep, sleeping, soundly sleeping, fast asleep, sound asleep, fast asleep. *Sleep on, sleep soundly and well, sleep, sleep soundly.*"

You now proceed with both local and by general passes *at distance* to abstract your influence (but not to awaken your now-sensitive) by moving your hands with fingers extended, slowly from his head to his fingers, both inside and outside the arms, also from the forehead down in front of the body to the pit of the stomach and then towards the knees. At the termination of each pass raise the hands (as described in practising the passes) and commence again. Continue these passes for some time after he has apparently fallen asleep.

The next step is to see what state the patient is in. The repose, the heavier breathing, are helpful indications; but should there be any doubt, gently raise one of the eyelids, when one of two things will happen— the subject will wake up, or will remain quiescent, showing only the white of the eye. He is in the hypnotic state. He is now in a position to receive *suggestion;* they are received by the subliminal self, fully appreciated and acted on.

A state of hypnosis being induced, one or other of the following signs will be noticed in the subject: "A dulness comes over the eyes and the eyelids gradually sink or close as the hypnotic influence takes effect. There is a rotatory upward motion of the eye-balls, as in natural sleep or approximation thereto. There is sometimes a tremour in the closing eyelids, which may or may not wholly cover the eyes. Should the eyes be open, their expression is—*expressionless.* The features are about as mobile as a mask. There is more or less torpor, arms and legs sluggish. The respirations will be quiet and heavy, and the pulse, as a rule, low and even. Consciousness varies with the depth of the state. The subject may remember all that has been said to him or may not, just as he is semi-somnolent, somnolent, somnambulistic or in a deeper state."

If you do not succeed at first, proceed at subsequent sittings as if you had no previous failure. The practical hypnotist knows the most difficult cases are overcome in the course of a few sittings. *That the effects of his suggestions are accumulative.* As soon as the obstructions of nervous restlessness, fear, anxiety, doubt in the subject are overcome, *success is assured.* When once you succeed in putting a person asleep, your power to do so will be enhanced; and your future percentages will increase in due proportion. These remarks apply to waking stage experiments, as well as any other in the direction of "New Thought Research."

That the subject is slow to respond, or be affected, should cause no uneasiness. Such cases turn out the very best and not only do they enter the state with surprising suddenness, but in case of patients, are rapidly cured. Tact, perseverance and patience on your part are bound to tell.

A subject may be refractory without meaning it. Temperament, fear, too much anxiety, state of health, inability to concentrate attention, etc.,—one or all combined may delay induction of hypnosis.

When you have obtained satisfactory evidence of sleep, it is advisable to try no experiments for the first 2 or 3 *sittings* beyond the following: Let him sleep on for some time, and then quietly wake him up. You may, however, facilitate matters by giving a *post-hypnotic suggestion* just before the termination of the experiment, assuring him that *he will enter more fully into the state at the next seance.*

AWAKENING THE SUBJECT.—Do not do this suddenly. You might spoil forever a good subject by so doing. Inform your subject that you are about to wake him up and say, "When you hear the word *three* you will be wide awake." Stand behind or before him and make slowly and then briskly upward passes (palms of the hands up) *in front of the face* and blow steadily on the forehead and say, "Now, one, two, *three. Awake,*" and your subject will awake much surprised and benefiitted by the sleep.

CHAPTER VI.

MODES OF PROCEDURE.

I propose in this chapter to give a few methods of inducing hypnosis adopted by some of the most eminent of hypnotists.

DR. BRAID'S MODE OF PROCEDURE.—"Take any bright object between the thumb and fore and middle fingers of the left hand; hold it from about 8 to 15 inches from the eyes at such a position above the forehead as may be necessary to produce the greatest possible strain upon the eyes and the eyelids, and enable the patient to maintain a steady, fixed stare at the object. The patient must be made to understand that he must keep the eyes steadily fixed on the object. It will be observed that, owing to the consensual adjustment of the eyes, the pupils will be at first contracted, they will shortly begin to dilate, and after they have done so to a considerable extent, and have assumed a very wary position, if the fore and middle fingers of the right hand, extended and a little separated, are carried from the object towards the eyes, most likely the eyelids will close involuntarily with a vibratory motion. If this is not the case, or the patient allows the *eye-balls to move,* desire him to begin again, giving him to understand that he is to allow the eyelids to close when the fingers are again carried to the eyes, but that the eye-balls *must* be kept fixed on the same position and the mind riveted to the *one idea* of the object held before the eyes."

(119)

In the hypnotic state the senses, with the exception of sight, are wonderfully exalted. Thus a subject who could not hear the ticking of a watch beyond 3 ft. when in his normal state, could do so when hypnotised at a distance of 35 ft. and walk towards it in a straight line, without any hesitation. Again, another subject (lady) was able to trace a rose by smell when held at a distance of 46 ft. from her.

PROFESSOR HEIDENHAM'S MODE OF PROCEDURE.—His processes are very simple and may be divided into two parts:

1. By monotonous stroking of the temples or nose.

2. By monotonous sounds, such as the ticking of a watch.

Experiment.—He placed 3 chairs with their backs against a table upon which rested a small watch. The chairs were occupied by 3 subjects, whose attention was directed (of course by continuous suggestion) to the monotonous ticking of the watch, while the hypnotist went on with local passes directed to the cranial region. Doubtless, all three fell asleep.

The methods adopted by Charcot, Mm. Baurru, Butot, Voisin and others are but modifications of the above. We will watch another case ere we close this chapter.

The hypnotist is a medical man. He is seated by a couch on which his patient lies. Necessary directions as to posture, attitude of mind, etc., have already been given to the patient. The forefinger of the right hand of the hypnotist is then directed to a little above and in front of the patient's eyes. The latter looks steadily at the tip of the finger presented to him and continues keeping it there. As the doctor is talking (suggestions) he quietly moves his finger backwards and then forwards and also slightly laterally to about 6 inches from the patient's eyes This causes a slight movement of the eye-balls with periodical squint eyes, and the patient is altogether unaware of it. The doctor goes on with his sleep suggestions in a quiet monotone:

"Now look steadily at my finger. Keep your eyes there; you will soon feel the influence; just keep your gaze fixed and steady at it. Don't mind anything else. Just look and listen. Your eyes are getting heavier and heavier every moment. They are tired and heavy, more and more tired; getting tired and heavy. The influence is on you now. You feel it, tired and heavy; tired and heavy. Your eyes are closing. Very tired and heavy, closing. Your eyes are closing, c-l-o-s-i-n-g, c-l-o-s-i-n-g. You cannot keep them open long. It is impossible. They are closing, closing. *You are going to sleep, to sleep, to sound sleep: to sound, sound sleep, go to sleep, very sound sleep,*" and so on with quiet repetition.

As this sleep talk is quietly kept up, the eyelids droop; the doctor quietly seizes the opportunity to brush them down close them, in fact, and then commences *local and occasional long passes* in conjunction with *sleep-suggestions:* "Your eyes are closed. Completely closed, closed, sleepy, closed; you will have no tendency to open them, sleep on. Sleep soundly, sleep, sleep, sleep on. You are sound asleep, asleep; sleeping soundly; from head to foot in sound sleep, fast asleep," and so on, repeating.

Watching the altered and heavy breathing or action of the eyelids, the doctor is satisfied that the patient is in a quiescent or suggestible state, and then he slightly raises his voice, assuming a commanding tone, thus:

"You are now completely under my control; you cannot open your eyes. It is impossible. However hard you may try, *you cannot open your eyes.* Your eyes are firmly closed. You are in very deep sleep now, soundly sleeping. Sleep on, it is very comfortable. You are enjoying undisturbed sleep, sleep on."

"You are fast asleep, soundly sleeping, asleep, asleep. Nothing can disturb your sleep, your excellent and refreshing sleep. No noise in the world can disturb you. In fact, you cannot hear any other voice except mine. All other voices are shut to you. You will not hear any noise, any other than my voice. You are under my control now. The whole world is shut to you. *You will hear my voice very distinctly*, my voice and mine alone. You hear my voice clearly and distinctly; isn't it? Yes, you will hear it very well. Sleep. Sleep well."

Then without further experimenting the doctor proceeds to give healing suggestions *carefully and deliberately—without monotone—in a clear, hopeful confident, distinct and emphatic voice.*

This part of the subject will meet with more attention under *"Suggestive Therapeutics."*

EXPERIMENTS IN THE SLEEPING STAGE.

After inducing *hypnosis* in your subject, you have practically very little to do by way of monotonous suggestions or passes. However, it is good to use occasional passes and suggestions conducive to sleep.

Under the influence of the operator, there is absolutely no end to the illusions and hallucinations which may be created in the subject's mind, and acted upon without question. Fertility of resource and direction are requisite in an entertainer more than the so-called extraordinary will-power to which success is so often attributed. A detailed list of experiments suitable for an entertainment will not serve any useful purpose here. However, I will touch upon a few interesting experiments just to show you what can be done. A very telling experiment is this: Here the subject has a really bad tooth, which is not, and can never be, of any use to him. Having thrown him to sleep, and further, having assured him (suggestion) that his whole body is insensible to pain, some well-known dentist may be requested to extract the tooth. The extraction will be a painless one and the experiment most interesting.

Never allow your subjects to eat or drink anything which can in any sense do them injury, nor allow abusive liberties to be taken with them under the pretence of proving that your entertainment is like Cæsar's wife, above suspicion.

You may catelepse your subject, make his body or any portion thereof as rigid as a board and unconscious to pain; this can be easily done by means of a few local passes, adding suitable suggestions. You may convert water into milk, tea or wine, and *vice versa,* and your subject will taste just the same as you suggest, and describe it as such. He may be made to fish or act the tailor or even the Emperor of India, all at your suggestion. You may even permit him to have his eyes open, suggesting that he would be still in sound sleep and could not see anything but as directed by you. A hat may be presented to him for a tiger and the terror excited will be most interesting.

There is something inexpressibly funny in seeing a sedate old man forget his sedateness and make passionate avowals of affection to a supposed young lady (who is another man dressed up for the purpose). The subject may personate some actor or deliver an address; caress a pillow for baby; use a walking-stick for a spoon; all this and a hundred more experiments may be done by *suggestion*. But what then, if this be all? Fortunately, this is not all, as has already been pointed out elsewhere. While hypnotic or mesmeric entertainments amuse, they may be used successfully to draw attention to the more special and scientific aspects of this grand subject—curative, telepathic, clairvoyant, etc.

NOTE.—Let your suggestions be wholesome, happy, healthy and beneficial, elevating character always. Never descend to practical jokes or to aught hurtful or unpleasant, simply to gratify your vanity, sense of the ridiculous or to amuse others, at the expense of your subject's health and happiness.

POST-HYPNOTIC SUGGESTION.—Suggestions that are given in the sleeping stage with the result that the experiments suggested take effect after the subject wakes up and in his normal senses, are said to be *post-hypnotic*.

The correction of bad habits is effected by *post-hypnotic suggestion*. Take, for example, a child given up to the stealing habit. Throw the child into a state of hypnosis and take it to a table whereon you have already placed a two-anna piece, and say, "You see this piece of money. If you quietly pocket it, it will serve to fetch you four oranges. You wish to put it in your pocket."

The child readily pockets it and you continue, "You are going to put it back on the table whence you took it; you are ashamed of your act. It is theft, pure and simple. If at any time hereafter you yield to the temptation, you will be ashamed of having committed theft and you will be anxious to return the object to its place. Indeed, you will never be tempted to steal." In simple language, varied and repeated to suit the case, the child is cured forever of any tendency to steal.

I close this chapter by quoting one out of many cases of moral perversion cured by Dr. Voisin by *Post-hypnotic suggestions*, abbreviated as follows:

"A lad of 16 was brought to Dr. Voisin at Saltpetriere on June 9, 1888. He was an utterly corrupt young rascal. He lied, played truant, was grossly indecent, trying to corrupt all with whom he came in contact. He had been, on account of his vices and unspeakable conduct, turned out of several institutions where he had been placed in the hope of cure and reform. Dr. Voisin's report on his vices cannot be repeated here, and consequently his case may be looked upon as hopelessly bad. He had certain physical defects— an internal squint of the left eye which exhibited haziness of the cornea and other defects. His general health was good. Dr. Voisis endeavoured to hypnotise him and succeeded after much difficulty to do so at the third sitting. When hypnosis had been produced, suggestions of reform were given, and received, with the result that improvement was made from the very beginning. By July 6 his whole character was changed. *All this was effected in little less than four weeks.* The desires to do evil were obliterated and those to do good were more and more manifested. He was no longer insubordinate to his mother, whose life had been rendered miserable by his utterly depraved and degenerate conduct. He now took a pleasure in pleasing his mother and expressed thanks to Dr. Voisin for the great change which had taken place."

Post-hypnotic Suggestion is the basis of all curative treatment.

N. B.—*Subject* means anybody brought under the influence or control of the Hypnotist. The word *Patient* has also been used in this Part in place of *Subject*, as most persons coming under the direction of the operator happen to be patients for treatment of certain diseases.

CHAPTER VII.

MESMERISM AND CLAIRVOYANCE.

MESMERISM deals with the theory and practice of "Animal Magnetism." The name is derived from Dr. Anthony Mesmer, the founder of the science. Hypnotism is a modern modification of the same. The chief distinction between hypnotism and mesmerism is that in the former we mainly rely on *suggestion* to produce the various results, whereas the latter is a more silent method of gaining the same ends by means of the fluid called "Animal Magnetism." The mesmerist recognizes that in order to act upon a patient there must be a connecting link of *sympathy* between them. This connecting link is not a creation of *suggestion* by which the phantasies and illusions of hypnotic patients are created, but a real link by which (moral, mental and physical) *sympathy* is thoroughly established between the mesmerist and his subject. This *sympathy or rapport* is effected by concentration of the *will* of the operator; the honest means to relieve pain and cure disease, then finds a ready channel for communication. With mesmerism, *clairvoyance* and the more advanced spiritual phenomena are possible; but these are seldom seen to gain ground with hypnotism.

The mesmeric and hypnotic states are frequently confounded with each other; but it must be remembered that they are quite distinct, if allied. In the former the subject has an inward *illuminated condition*—a

strong moral and spiritual individuality—a penetration
and clear-headedness marked and distinct; the latter is
a creation of circumstances.

MESMER'S FLUID-THEORY—ANIMAL MAGNETISM.—
"This fluid exercises an immediate action on the nerves
with which it embodies itself, and produces in the
human body phenomena similar to those produced by
the load-stone, that is, polarity and inclination. Hence
the name *Animal Magnetism.*

"This fluid flows with the greatest quickness from
body to body, acts at a distance, and is reflected by the
mirror-like light, and it is strengthened and propagated
by sound. There are animated bodies which exercise
an action directly opposite to Animal Magnetism. Their
presence alone is capable of destroying the effects of
magnetism. This power is a positive power.

"By means of Animal Magnetism, we can effect an
immediate cure of the nervous diseases and a mediate
cure of all diseases."

HOW TO CULTIVATE ANIMAL MAGNETISM.—The
method is just the same as was described in Part I for
hypnotism. In fact, the principles explained there
constitute the key to all the processes carried on under
the "New Thought Research."

DIFFERENT STAGES IN MESMERISM.—In addition to
the four stages that we saw under hypnotism we have
here two more, *viz.:*

5th Stage.. The Lucid Somnambulistic Stage.—
Here we have clear vision or clairvoyance (including
thought-transference, intro-vision and pre-vision) manifested. In this state, the subject is able to measure his
own internal mental and bodily state, and those of a
third party when placed *en rapport* with him. In cases
of diseases, he will prescribe suitable remedies and fore-
shadow the termination of the attack.

6th Stage. The Independent or Spiritual Stage.—
In this the subject's vision is not limited by space or

sympathy; he passes wholly, as in the last stage partially, beyond the sole control of the operator.

All persons can be brought under the first four stages; but there are only a limited number (about 5 in 1,000) that pass into the 5th or 6th stage. These adapted to the higher phases of clairvoyance, thought-transference, etc., would be degraded or injured (*i. e.*, their powers obscured), should they be put to the buffooneries of the public platform; and those most suited to public entertainments seldom exhibit any aptitude for the higher phenomena. It must be remembered that these phenomena depend more upon certain nervous and psychic conditions in the sensitive than in the mesmeric powers of direction possessed by the operator. There should therefore be no forcing of results.

METHOD OF PROCEDURE.

The following method presents, in its simplest form, the procedure adopted by the best class of mesmerists. It is due to Captain James, the most successful mesmerist since the days of Dr. Elliotson, whose friend and pupil he was.

He writes: "It is recommended that the mesmerist should direct his patient either to place himself in an easy-chair or lie down on a couch, so that he may be perfectly at ease. The mesmeriser then either standing or seated opposite his patient, should place his hand with extended fingers, over the head, and make passes slowly down to the extremities, as near as possible to the face and the body without touching the patient, taking care at the end of each pass to close his hand until he returns to the head, when he should extend his fingers and proceed as before. It is also useful after making several of these passes to point the fingers close to the patient's eyes, which procedure, in many cases, has more effect than the passes. This simple process should be continued for about 20 minutes at the first *seance,* and may be expected to produce more or less effect accord-

ing to the susceptibility of the patient. Should the
operator perceive any signs of approaching sleep, he
should persevere with the passes until the eyes close,
and should he then observe a quivering of the eyelids he may be pretty certain that his efforts will be
successful.

"Sometimes slow breathing, or placing the hand on
the forehead, will deepen the sleep; but the beginner
should as a rule, avoid concentrating the mesmeric
force on the head or region of the heart, and confine
himself as much as possible to the passes *aux grands
courants*, as the French writers term them, *i. e.*, the
long, slow passes from the head to the feet. Should
the above described signs of mesmeric coma not declare
themselves at the end of 20 or 30 minutes, the mesmeriser should ask the patient whether he felt any
peculiar sensation during the process, and if so, whether
they were more apparent during the passes or when the
fingers were pointed at the eyes. By these inquiries he
will soon learn the best method of mesmerising applicable to each particular case, and he should not be
disheartened if he does not succeed in producing marked
effects at the first or even after successive *seances*.
Pain may be removed and diseases cured or greatly
alleviated without the production of sleep, and many
patients succumb at length who have for many weeks
been apparently unaffected and proof against all the
resources of the mesmeriser.

"Supposing sleep at length induced, the next and
very important question is how to awaken the patient.
With most sensitives this is a very easy process, for
merely blowing or fanning over the head and face with
a few transverse passes will at once dispel sleep. Should,
however, the patient experience a difficulty in opening
his eyes, then with the tips of his thumbs the operator
should rub firmly and briskly over the eyebrows from
the root of the nose outwards towards the temples, and
finish by blowing or fanning, taking special care before
leaving the patient that, judging from the expression

of his eyes and other signs, he has evidently returned to the normal state. As a rule, the patient should not be left until the operator is perfectly satisfied that he is wide wake.

"There are certain cases, however, where the sensitives should be allowed to sleep for 2 or 3 hours or even more, and particularly when lengthened sleep has been prescribed by the patients themselves. Care must be taken to ascertain that they can be left alone with impunity. The majority may be, but there are cases where the operator should not be absent during the sleep. With a little observation, the mesmeriser should be able to distinguish between such cases, and learn to adapt his treatment according to the peculiar temperament or constitution of each patient.

"The power of acting on or impressing the patient's mind may be carried into and continued in the normal or waking stage, and might be used with good effect in the treatment of dipsomania and other morbid habits, so that the patient would in many cases, in consequence of the impressions made during his sleep, be led to entertain an actual disgust at the mere smell of alcoholic liquor.

"The patient during his sleep can frequently give valuable directions to his mesmeriser, both as to the best methods of mesmerising him and the most effective means of terminating the sleep. In some rare cases the sleep is so prolonged in spite of all the operator's efforts to dispel it, that he is alarmed, and the patient becomes affected in his fears. *Above all things, the mesmeriser should preserve his presence of mind,* and may be assured that the longest sleep will end spontaneously.

"It may as well be observed in this place that *the patient should not be touched by anyone but his mesmeriser,* unless he wishes it, or at least gives his consent. He can, perhaps, bear the touch of certain individuals and may express a repugnance to be touched by others, and this quite irrespective of attachment or repulsion with regard to those individuals in his normal state. With most sensitives it is quite immaterial who or how many people touch them; but there are occasionally cases when, by so touching them, a very distressing state, called *'Cross Mesmerism,'* is produced, and the more particularly in the cases of persons who are naturally highly nervous, and, perhaps, hysterical. It is in these cases of cross-mesmerism that we most often find a difficulty in determining the sleep."

CLAIRVOYANCE.

CLAIRVOYANCE means "clear-seeing" or "soul sight," whereby the subject is enabled to see much that is hidden with sudden and startling clearness; clairvoyant subjects can be made to travel, visit places of interest and describe the places and people and report to you what they do and say. He will further be able to relate with wonderful accuracy the history of absent people (living or dead) by means of the *influence* still left on some old relic, such as a ring or gem. He can discover hidden things. There are authenticated instances of valuable mines having been discovered by clairvoyance. It is a well known historical fact that Mr. Wm. Denton discovered gold mines in Australia and also copper mines in Canada, through his wife. She was also of immense help to him in his scientific investigations.

Clairvoyance, as already pointed out elsewhere, is a normal possession. You cannot create it; but you can progressively develop and intensify powers of clairvoyance where they already exist. There should be no forcing of results or any hot-house planting about it. *There must be no hurry.*

Woman, for many reasons, makes a better clairvoyant subject than man. The best sensitives have been women from about 15 to 25, whose organisations were healthy, refined and pure, and who believed in the reality of the soul and things spiritual. Male sensitives are best for scientific and business purposes; females for literary, inspirational and previsional experiments. The very best sensitives are very difficult to get under control at first.

How to Cultivate Clairvoyance.—Place your subject in the *mesmeric sleep* sufficiently deep to be entirely lost to all external consciousness. Carefully subdue the physical and outward *senses* in the sensitive. He will in this state be a clear-headed, far-seeing and self-possessed being—having a distinct and exalted individuality —from whom you may learn a good deal about yourself, about the powers of the human soul and the best modes of procedure applicable to perfect his condition.

Commence by putting him some questions gently and judiciously—not hastily or suggestively—to know how and how long he wishes to sleep, what he feels and experiences in this state, and what he desires to be done in order to improve it, whether he perceives any *light* in his brain, and the location and the character of the same, whether in the forehead, crown of the head or at the sides; whether he can look into his own organisation or that of yours or any others placed in *sympathy* with him; what the nature of his power of vision is; if he is in a position to travel and visit distant places for you and describe the people and their actions there. In this way you will go on from day to day ascertaining what powers he possesses. See how far he perceives your intentions, thoughts or wishes—unexpressed by you. Always be kind and firm.

For this class of experiments the sittings should be arranged at a regular hour daily. In most cases an hour's duration will be long enough for each sitting.

Experiment as follows: Give him a playing card and see how far he is able to read and describe it as by telling its colour, what suit it belongs to, etc. Your sensitive's descriptions, however faulty at first, will become correct in the main, then singularly accurate, then marvellously so. Next you may gradually increase the distance between him and the card; you can then intensify the conditions by merely presenting him the back of the card only.

The following experiment is interesting: Give your subject a pocket-knife, kerchief or other much used article belonging to a third party whom you do not know, but whose appearance, disposition, character, etc., may be vouched for subsequently by trusted parties, and ask your sensitive what are his feelings and sensations experienced by him through the articles placed in his possession; if the questions are carefully and judiciously put, it is more than likely he will give out a vague and broken idea of the person whose articles he has. At subsequent sittings the power to diagnose surroundings, history, etc., will be enhanced, and his spiritual perceptions will be increased to such an extent (by proper directions) that he will be able to describe the character and life of the person concerned (from the very childhood upwards) with startling accuracy and in detail.

As this India manual is addressed to the student, rather than the novelty hunter, with this parting word— "Persevere with New Thought Science"—these pages shall be brought to a conclusion.

THE END OF BOOK TWO.

INDIA'S
HOOD UNVEILED

SOUTH INDIA MYSTERIES

𝔅𝔬𝔬𝔨 𝔗𝔥𝔯𝔢𝔢

INDIA'S HOOD UNVEILED

SOUTH INDIA MYSTERIES

𝕭𝖔𝖔𝖐 𝕿𝖍𝖗𝖊𝖊

STUDENT'S ADVANCED COURSE

HINDU MAGNETISM, HINDU HYPNOTISM, HINDU MES-
MERISM, HINDU SUGGESTIVE THERAPEUTICS, HINDU
PSYCHO-THERAPEUTICS, HINDU MIND READING,
HINDU TELEPATHY, HINDU MAGNETIC HEAL-
ING, HINDU DEVELOPMENT OF THE WILL,
HINDU CLAIRVOYANCE, ETC.

BY A NATIVE OF

SOUTH INDIA

Published exclusively in the United States by

THE de LAURENCE COMPANY

Chicago, Ill., U. S. A., 1910

Preface to Book Three

It is intended by this work to sketch in a concise manner what the possibilities of the human mind are, and how to develop and practically employ the same in every-day life.

The science is no abstraction, but something to be practiced by everybody and in all places, and made an efficient help to that noblest of all studies—the study of MAN. To make this grand subject of mental philosophy readily understood by all and as readily applied, it is written in ordinary every-day language and may limp a little here and there. For none of these faults do I offer an apology to my readers. I ask them to take it as it is—as something more than a mere introduction to a most interesting and important subject.

It is desirable to consider the subject under six distinct heads, if allied. The present volume embraces (1) The Machinery of the "New Thought Science," (2) Hypnotism, and (3) Mesmerism and Clairvoyance. It is intended, in due course, to issue a companion volume comprising (4) Suggestive Therapeutics and Magnetic Treatment, (5) Auto-suggestion and (6) Telepathy; thus completing the course.

Theoretical discussions will be avoided as far as possible, and I shall confine myself to simple practical rules throughout.

(139)

I make no pretense, however, to originality, as the whole work, with the exception of some of my own experimental results, is essentially a compilation from various authorities, too numerous to mention.

CHAPTER I.

STUDENT'S ADVANCED COURSE.

MAGNETIC HEALING.

Reader! we have already initiated you into the mysteries of Occultism and have made you grasp the elementary principles of what the Will can do. By the aid of this Will man has the faculty of exercising over his fellow men a salutary influence, in directing towards them, the vital principle. This faculty has been termed as Magnetism. As it is not possible to surmise how one body can act upon another at a distance, without the aid of a medium, we are compelled to suppose that there is something that emanates from him who magnetises to the magnetised. We call this which sustains life in us, the *Magnetic Fluid.*

We do not know its nature and even its very existence has not been proved; but everything occurs as it did exist and we believe we are permitted in sustaining the existence of such a fluid.

Thus the basis of all is "Will"; secondly, confidence in our own power, and thirdly and lastly, benevolence or the desire of doing good. One of these qualities may create the other in course of time; but to have an energetic and salutary effect, the three should be combined. If the desire of doing good be not initial, there will be some effects; but they will be irregular. Further, as the fluid that emanates from the Magnetiser exercises

(141)

a *physical* influence, and in course of time an effect upon the normal conditions also of the patient, it becomes necessary that the magnetiser ought to be in good health and one worthy of esteem for the uprightness of his mind, the purity of his sentiments and the honesty of his character.

Before undertaking the treatment of a patient, you ought to examine yourself by asking whether you can continue it and whether the patient or those who have influence over him will put any obstacles in the way. You should not undertake it if you feel any repugnance or fear to catch the disease. To act efficaciously, you should take a great care in the patient; you should take an interest in him and have the desire and hope of curing or at least relieving him.

The power of magnetising or that of doing good to your fellow creatures by the influence of your will, by the medium of that which sustains your health and life, being the most pleasant and delightful gift God has endowed on man, you ought to regard it as an act which demands the greatest purity of attention. Hence it is a sort of profanation to magnetise for amusement through curiosity or through the pleasure of exhibiting wonderful effects. They, who demand experiments to see a spectacle know not what they demand; but you ought to know it respect yourself and preserve your dignity.

SCEPTICAL PATIENTS.

If you chance to have a sceptical patient, do not worry yourself in trying to convince him what you can do. Do not argue with him under any consideration. But directly proceed with your work and in course of time he will be sorry for what he has said and you will be respected for your tolerance, judgment and ability.

If your patient chances to be under the advice of any Medical man, do not advise him to discontinue medicine. Never oppose Medical men. Plainly impress your patient that your treatment can do no harm. Best results can be obtained when you have the patient close his eyes during the treatment. Some, even of the eminent men, do instruct you to profess and work in a mysterious manner (i. e.), to make an examination of the pulse and to close your eyes and seem apparently to think deeply under great mental strain. But we do not advise you to lead such a dubious life and we teach you how to examine the pulse and to diagnose diseases. No other institute gives you the symptoms of the various diseases you may come across, but simply names them.

THE PULSE, BREATHING AND RESPIRATION.

Certain acts connected with the pulse, the breathing or respiration, the temperature of the body and the tongue are the most important points to be borne in mind when attempting to discover the nature, or to treat diseases.

The pulse is caused by the beating of the arteries which convey the blood to all parts of the body from the heart. It can be felt wherever there is an artery near the surface, such as in the neck or thigh, but for convenience sake it is felt in the wrist. The generally accepted number of beats per minute in the healthy state, according to age, are:

> Till end of first year..............140
> Till end of third year.............120 to 100
> Till end of sixth year.............100 to 90
> From 7th to 14th year............. 90 to 75
> From 14th to 21st year............ 85 to 75
> From 21st to 68th year............ 75 to 65
> Old age .... 85 to 70

This may vary in some cases and there are some persons who have extraordinary slow or fast beatings without the least deviation from health. Generally if the pulse is slow or fast by dozen beats without previous bodily exertion, there is something wrong; if higher, the symptoms of fever; if lower, a want of vitality. It is only after a long experience you can properly learn the pulse.

(1)   A large, soft and frequent pulse indicates febrile disease.

(2)   A frequent hard and full pulse-inflammations.

(3)   An increase in pulse after a meal or in the evening-hectic fever.

(4)   Irregular, jerking or vibratory pulse-heart diseases.

(5)   A weak, thread-like pulse, very dangerous cases, as cholera, etc.

THE BREATH.

In breathing there should be no difference in the movement of the chest. The average breathing is about one for every four beats of the pulse. Here are also exceptional cases. As in the pulse, if the breathing is higher it would indicate some malady in the lungs; if lower, debility or loss of vital power or nervous shock.

Understanding the breathing also requires a long practice and knack, and inferences can be made as to the diseases, even from the smell of breath.

1.   A faint apple-like smell or odour indicates Diabetes.

2.   A sour smell, Gastric disorders.

3.   A smell of sulphurated hydrogen, Dyspepsia.

4.   An ammoniacal or urinous odour, Bladder and Kidney affections.

5.   A sour and urinous smell, Excess in spirituous liquors.

THE TONGUE.

Just as the face is the index of the mind, so the tongue is the index of the health of the body. Hence, a careful examination of the tongue is necessary in almost all cases. A few of its peculiarities are given below:

1. A pale, white, flabby tongue indicates a weak, debilitated condition of the system.

2. A florid redness of the tongue, Plethora.

3. A purplish color, diseases of the chest.

4. A furred tongue, some kind of febrile affection.

5. A cream-like fur-inflammations, acute rheumatism and fever.

6. Thick brown black coating and a dry parched and cracked tongue, loss of motion.

7. Bright red points on the tongue, scarlet fever.

8. Yellow, Jaundice.

9. With red edges furred in the middle, Dyspepsia.

10. Tremulous, Intemperance or the abuse of drugs.

In addition to the above the various symptoms of loss of appetite, cough, delirium, fever, giddiness, headache, pain, palpitations, shivering, sore-throat, thirst, urinary condition, vomiting, etc., exist as reference to the diseases.

THE WARM BREATH.

In Magnetic Healing, the effects are mostly brought about by the agency of passes and massage. A certain amount of suggestion is also used. The passes are in themselves suggestions. Your very mode of treating the patient and moving towards him will have a salutary effect upon him.

The breath is the main factor in the treatment of all diseases. The heat produced by it has a wonderful soothing effect. You may produce the "Warm breath" by keeping your mouth in a position to utter the word "Haw." Fold a handkerchief fourfold in thickness and place it over the seat of pain, and keep your mouth over that and blow hard and the hot breath charged with your magnetic fluid will pass through into the system; you should practice this, placing the handkerchief upon your arm itself and blowing. Hot breath should not be applied in sores or burns, where you should use only cold breath.

Cold breath is caused by your keeping the mouth at a distance of one foot from the affected part in position to say "Oh" and expelling the inhaled air. Have the mouth nearly closed, so that the breath given out may come out with some compressed force of the lips. Here you may dispense with the aid of kerchief and simply blow upon the bare flesh of the affected part. This will give the patient a very refreshing and soothing effect upon the affected part.

In blowing either warm or cold breath, commence to blow about 6 inches above from the seat of disease and continue to about 6 inches down the affected part.

HEALING PASSES.

The word pass denotes the movements made by the hand in passing over the body, either by touching slightly or by being at distance. There are many kinds of passes employed in Magnetic Healing. They are:

Long passes (or Longitudinal passes, as they are called) at contact or distance are made from the top of the patient's head to the extremities of the feet. By this pass we distribute equally the magnetic fluid into all the organs of the body. But the fluid has naturally a tendency to accumulate in such parts as may be in need of it.

SHORT PASSES.

Short drawing passes (or Local passes) are made about six inches from above the seat of pain to about six inches down; and when you come to the affected part, accumulate and concentrate the magnetic fluid upon it; and then draw it down to about 6 or 7 inches to the extremities of the part, as the magnetic fluid, when motion is given to it, draws along with it the blood the humors and the cause of the complaint.

To concentrate the fluid the fingers of your hands united to a point should be brought near towards the person's affected part and should be held there for one or two minutes.

QUIVERING PASSES.

This is done by quivering your hands with your fingers extended as they pass along the body; while you do this, a good deal of magnetic fluid or nerve energy is passing from your hands to the patient's affected part. When you make this "will" determinedly, "all your pain will entirely disappear; you will feel decided relief all over your body."

TRANSVERSE PASSES.

These are employed to scatter the superabundant fluid that might have been charged upon the patient by the long passes. To make the transverse passes raise your hands in front of the patient's head and as you make downward passes, move your hands with your fingers slightly curved, in a zig-zag way (*i. e.*) from the face, move the hands in a straight line to the heart region, then to his right side, then to his left, and so on, until you reach the toes. Then throw hands away.

DEMESMERISING PASSES.

Demesmerising passes or Upward passes, as they are called, should be used in awakening the mesmerised subjects. No suggestions or clapping of hands to be used, as with hypnotic subjects.

Passes should always be made lightly and slowly. Downward passes should always be made from the affected part and you should throw hands at the end of each pass, when, you should shake your hands as if you try to throw off some sticky substance from your hands. No decided opinion can be given as to the exact time one may occupy in curing any disease. Some apparently dangerous cases can be cured in one or two treatments, and minor cases, occupy even weeks and months.

Many hopeless cases have been successfully treated by
Magnetic Healers. On no circumstance discontinue a
case when you have once undertaken, as you may often
cure when you least expect it. Observe as a rule to
wash your hands with cold water and soap at the end
of each and every treatment.

MAGNETISED WATER.

Magnetised water has a most remedial effect in the
treatment of all diseases of human nature. It can
be taken in as a tonic and can even be used in baths,
either ordinary or vapour.

The magnetised water, as a tonic acts therapeutically
and directly at the organisation of the patient through
the blood circulation.

HOW TO MAGNETISE WATER.

Hold a glass tumbler full of filtered fresh spring water
or distilled water (preferred) in the palm of your left
hand and hold the fingers of your right, over it pointing
them down on the surface of the water. Gaze intently
into the water and think what you wish to effect with a
great determination. For instance, you may mentally
suggest. "This water will act as a tonic; it will sooth
your system; by this, you will completely recover from
your disease."

"Will" some such suggestions as may suit the case and
so that the patient may be able to understand them if
he heard. It is also better to breathe "cold breath" upon
the water before it is used.

Thus habituate yourself to magnetising various sec-
ondary objects for the patient that serve to promote the
health; for instance, bandages of wool, diet, water, as
these are advantageous in the treatment.

THE DAILY USE OF WATER.

The application of water or vapour comes under term

bath. The daily use of water to the body either by means of the sponge or plunge is one of the best and most easily applied rules of hygiene. The bath may be classified Cold, Tepid, Hot, Simple and Medicated. Baths may be either general or local. For example, the sitz or hip bath and foot bath are local; a bath is termed general, when the whole body with the exception of the head is immersed.

After a cold bath the body should be well warmed either by currents of hot air or other means as any exposure to cold winds would result in danger. During the cold weather, as it is not possible to warm the body through hot air, a warm foot bath can be advantageously given.

All physicians agree that a hot foot bath is one of the most efficacious means of restoring warmth and circulation to the extremities.

How to Give a Foot Bath in Bed.—Lay a large bath towel smoothly in the bed just about the place where the knees of the patient come. Then prepare a foot-tub ¾ full of warm water of the right temperature, and slide the foot-tub in beneath the covers, letting it rest upon the towel you have previously arranged. Help your patient to lie on his back and ask him to draw up his feet by bending his knees so that the feet will rest in the tub placed about where the knees were. Now cover the top of the tub by another towel so as to prevent the steam dampening the bedsheets. Allow him to remain for 15 minutes. Then remove the tub away and let the patient's feet rest upon the towel. Then wipe the feet dry and remove the towel. The whole thing is so simple that you can easily administer it at any time.

The temperature of the various baths may be stated as follows:

Tepid Bath .... 85 to 95 degrees
Warm Bath .... 95 to 102 degrees
Hot Bath .... 106 to 110 degrees

The vapour bath may be applied by the aid of a suitable apparatus when the patient is in bed or by sitting in an enclosed space into which the steam is freely admitted.

The medicated vapour baths are those into which chemical substances are introduced, such as Carbonate of Soda, Salt or Vinegar.

The Turkish bath is not only one of the most invigorating, but also one of the most enjoyable which we possess. After a day's fatigue it is wonderful how refreshing a Turkish bath is. It is however very necessary to use every precaution, in the way of having the body cooled thoroughly before going again into the open air. Moreover, the Turkish bath possesses curative properties of a very high importance in many diseases such as Neuralgia, Rheumatism, Paralysis, Dropsical swellings, Chronic diseases of the lung and affections of the Digestive organs. The wonderful part it plays is simply astonishing. To treat the above mentioned diseases, it is very necessary to possess a Turkish bath cabinet of your own; write to us and we shall be pleased to procure one at a moderate cost.

RULES FOR TREATMENT.

In the treatment of all diseases a strict observation of the following details should be adhered to:

(1) Comfortable position of the patient either in sitting posture or a convenient lying on the bed.

(2) Closing of the patient's eyes.

(3) Placing of the handkerchief on the seat of pain and application of "warm breath."

(4) Giving "passes" for a time, say 5 to 15 minutes as the case may seem to require after the removal of the kerchief over the affected portions of the body.

(5) At the close of each treatment, ask the patient to take a long breath and expel (inhaling by the nostrils and exhaling by the mouth) quickly; at that time make passes over the affected part and bring down your hands and throw off at the exact time he expels the breath.

This should be repeated thrice at least at each treatment. The treatment if given directly on the flesh is better; in cases, where this is not possible, have the patient cover the body in a thin sheet. If you want to achieve quick and beneficent results, insist on treating direct over the flesh, if you find the treatment over the sheet a little encouraging. The whole treatment should not take more than 20 minutes; 5 to 10 minutes is always sufficient. When covered, the breath is not necessary. The breath will always give you a beneficent result. You should have a definite way of procedure. If you show any signs of forgetfulness or hesitate, then your patient's confidence in you will be totally destroyed and all your efforts will bear no fruit. By your methods of procedure you should inspire a sort of confidence in the patients. Your talk should be regulated in such a way as to enhance the confidence created in him. You should speak to him of the various diseases you have cured and tell him that you also hope to cure him.

Do not make any promise or specify any time for recovery. You should impress on him well that he will be benefited by your treatment, as you know what a potent factor the mind is and what its powers are. If your patient's mind is polluted with such delusions, that he cannot be cured, he will die, etc., the probable ultimatum is:

It should be borne in mind that magnetic treatment takes some time to show its effect. You cannot expect an instantaneous result. You should also impress the patient of the fact.

HOW TO APPEAR BEFORE A PATIENT.

Always make it a point never to appear before a patient when you are in a temper, passion or any disquietude of the mind, nor allow them to visit you in any of the above states; for, a violation of this rule will make them partake of the then-condition of your mind.

Do not reveal your troubles to your patient; for, that will make him form a very low opinion of your powers.

When a patient visits you, always appear in his presence with a pleasant smile.

Then keep your eyes fixed upon the root of the patient's nose as long as you can, when you are with him. Keep repeating mentally the following suggestions all the time you are "gazing" at the patient, "I can cure you; you will feel better; all your pains and sufferings will completely leave you; you will notice a very good change in your condition; you will have perfect confidence in my ability; you will like my presence more and more."

In this way, you can establish a telepathic sympathy and rapport with your patient which is a sure basis of a certain cure.

CHAPTER II.

HOW TO TREAT DIFFERENT DISEASES.

We will now proceed to give you instructions in the exact *modus operandi* of magnetic healing of the various diseases as far as practicable and their symptoms.

ABSCESS.

Abscess is applied to a painful and inflammed swelling, which, generally after removing a slow cover, terminates in a discharge of a yellowish creamy fluid known as *pus* or generally the "matter." This may occur in any part of the body and may either be externally or internally. The internal organs it most affects are the brain and liver.

Treatment.—Examine the case patiently and give for 5 minutes a few "passes at distance" commencing 6 inches from above the seat of disease and continue down to 6 inches and throw hands away. Then apply warm breath 4 or 5 times over the seat of pain. A slow cleansing of the affected part, with warm water by the aid of a syringe, will be extremely useful. Then slightly massage the affected part and give one or two vapour baths.

ACIDITY.

This is a frequent symptom of indigestion and often an accompaniment of chronic Rheumatism and gout. This is due to an excess of gastric juice in the stomach.

The symptoms are: Pain and burning at the pit of the stomach, flatulence, and an acid taste in the mouth.

Treatment.—In such cases the diet should be a very light one. The patient should be made to take some exercise or other to quicken the digestion. Have the patient stand up, if convenient, and ask him to close his eyes. Begin to make "passes at contact" with both hands from the sides of the body down to the pit of the stomach. Do this for 10 minutes. Then massage well the stomach region for 5 minutes. In massaging, your hands should take the direction of the movements of the hands of a clock. Then apply warm breath over the whole stomach region 4 or 5 times. Then suggest in a positive tone. "All your stomach troubles will entirely soon disappear; after each treatment you will feel better." Then ask him to take in a slow long breath and exhale it quickly. Let him do this 5 times and then open his eyes.

After a treatment or two successive vapour baths as referred to in the latter portion, if administered properly, will be of a great use in the quick relief of the patient's disease.

AGUE.

Ague or intermittent or Malarial fever is a periodical complaint which comes at definite intervals.

Symptoms.—It commences with a feeling of general lassitude, a sensation of weight in the region of the stomach, and a chilly sensation which rapidly develops into actual shivering and chattering of the teeth. When this disease appears to be at its height, the colour of the skin becomes livid and the body presents a shrivelled appearance. The circulation is feeble and the mucous surfaces become pallid, and sometimes actual stupor or convulsions may supervene. There appear shooting pains throughout the head and limbs. This cold stage will shortly be accompanied by intense heat and flushing of the whole body, when the pulse becomes quick and bounding, followed by a throbbing headache, hot skin, intense thirst, thickly coated tongue, and dark coloured urine. This stage is followed by a sweating stage, when copious perspiration gives the patient a rapid relief. All these above symptoms may again develop in 24, 48 or 72 hours or at longer periods as the case may be.

For treatment see under *Fevers*.

ALCOHOLISM.

Symptoms.—This is chiefly the result of over-indulgence in alcohol. The earlier stages are vomiting, especially in the morning, tremulousness of the hands, noises in the head, bad dreams, giddiness, tenderness of the feet, and piles. The very appearance of the person suffering from this complaint, tells of the man.

Treatment.—Put the patient into a deep sleep and suggest, "When I awaken you, all your desire for liquor will leave you; you will not require this stimulant; you will be disgusted with it; you will not like the smell of it; the very sight of it will be very hateful to you; you will not allow any body to tempt you; you will positively refuse to take a drink under any and all circumstances; every day you will become more disgusted with it; but it will not make you nervous to stop; every day you will require less" Give these suggestions 8 or 10 times in a positive tone. Treat him daily until entire relief.

ANÆMIA.

This represents more or less the lack of blood and its characteristic principle is poorness of blood. Its causes are numerous, the principal being insufficient diet, want of sunlight, fresh air and exercise, which in time lead to loss of appetite, excessive mental work, worry, etc.

Symptoms.—The skin becomes pale and in dark complexions presents a sallow appearance; palpitation of the heart; poor appetite; and puffiness about the face, legs and ankles being the chief symptoms.

Treatment.—Careful attention to diet and the daily evacuation of the bowels are the most essential things to be attended to. This is a very dangerous disease and if not remedied in time, would lead to sad consequences. This is more or less incurable to medicine. This can be treated very successfully only by the aid of "suggestion" and "hot bath." The suggestions should be specific as to the complaint. Such a system of treatment will effect a speedy cure.

APOPLEXY.

Symptoms.—This is a kind of fit in which the patient falls to the ground, deprived of senses and motion and lies like one who is in a deep sleep. The pulse will be full and slow, the face flushed and breathing laboured. The pupils, either one or both, may become dilated. Generally, convulsions of one side of the body may occur and stand for ever as in Paralysis. The foregoing symptoms are giddiness, nausea, sickness, fainting-feelings, headache, constipation, scanty urine, loss of memory, bleeding of the nose, double vision, confusion of ideas, faltering speech and numbness of the extremities, etc., together with sudden paralysis of one side of the body or of one leg or arm only. The patient may not be able to move the affected part or move with the greatest difficulty.

Treatment.—First lay open or loosen any tight clothing of the body. Slightly raise his head or put him in a recumbent position and apply pounded ice or cold water to his head. Keep the feet in hot water for a short time—say for 10 minutes—and then bottles filled with hot water should be applied to them. Rub your hands firmly and apply them over the calves and limbs of the leg after carefully brushing them with a towel. During the whole operation the body should be kept in a horizontal position. The knees may hang down. *Have the head and shoulders propped towards the right side.* Free ventilation should be allowed but not too much light. Do not allow anybody to be at his side during treatment except under extraordinary circumstances; then, too, do not allow more than one or two. If the fit occurs after the meal the patient may feel an inclination to vomit, if so, let him vomit. Under other conditions vomiting should not be encouraged.

After a time the patient may recover from the fit and he might have lost the use of an arm or a leg of one side of the body and at times even the speech may also be lost and some of the muscles also affected.

After some days put the subject into deep hypnosis and treat by suggestive therapeutics. (Vide Paralysis.) This is a disease which is beyond the power of medicine.

LOSS OF APPETITE.

This occurs in digestion, fever, and in inflammations, etc., and this is more or less a symptom of disease. This can be treated only by suggestive therapeutics. Put the patient into deep sleep and suggest "you will have good appetite in future; whatever food you take will easily digest, etc." Repeat similar suggestions 10 or 12 times and awaken him.

ASTHMA.

This is a paroxysmal disease which many are subject to. The attacks come on suddenly and last from 10 minutes to 3 or 4 hours; the appearance of such persons is characterised by thinness, round shoulders, anxious expression, hollow cheek, hoarse voice and habitual cough.

Treatment.—During the attack the patient should be kept sitting up. If severe, he may be placed in an easy chair, with some raised support in front, with a pillow to rest his elbows. Massage thoroughly the spine and give "passes at distance" for 10 minutes over it. Pressure with the thumb on the arteries of the arm will do a great deal of benefit. Blow hot breath on the chest and the spine and make passes over it, quivering over those parts with nervous energy. Do this for 3 minutes. Then ask him to inhale and exhale 5 times. After each treatment give a vapour bath to the patient for 15 minutes.

ATROPHY.

This is caused by want of proper food at proper time; so there is a constant lack of nerve energy in the affected parts. This can be effectively cured by the application of massage, suggestions and vapour bath.

BLEEDING.

In Bleeding, the patient should be kept cool. Ice can be administered often. Put him into Hypnosis and give apt suggestions to counteract the nature of this disease. While under treatment a good nutritious food is absolutely necessary for the patient.

BRONCHITIS.

This is an inflammation of the mucous membrane lining the air cells of the chest and it usually arises from cold. This may be acute or chronic in its character affecting one or both lungs throughout or a portion of these organs, generally the upper lobes. This disease is generally prevalent in young children and old people. This complaint is greatly aggravated by indigestion.

Symptom.—Fever, headache, a feeling of tightness about the chest, impeded respiration, perpetual wheezing cough, and general restlessness.

Treatment.—Seat the patient on a chair. Make "passes at contact" over the chest and spine for 10 minutes and throw hands away. Massage the chest and the back of the patient for 5 minutes and blow 5 hot breaths over the above said parts.

Then give vapour bath thrice a week. In giving vapour bath, put a teaspoonful of powered camphor in the pan with water and boil it well before seating the patient within the bath cabinet.

COLIC.

This is a painful spasmodic contraction of a muscular coat of the bowels, particularly that of the large bowels or colon. The characteristic symptom of colic is pain coming on in paroxysms which last for a shorter or longer period, and then gradually pass away only however, to recur within a short time.

Treatment—The pain can be relieved by suggestions. Apply hot breath over the abdomen. Then make passes over it for 10 minutes.

CONSTIPATION.

Symptoms.—It renders the individual more susceptible to infectious diseases. It interferes with the digestion. It interrupts the excreting power of different organs such as the liver, the kidneys, and the skin. It has a most pernicious effect upon the nervous system, causing depression of spirits, irritability of temper, disturbed and unrefreshing sleep and an undue sensibility to cold.

Treatment.—Have the patient sit down or better stand up. Make passes with both of your hands from the sides of his body over the abdomen to the lower regions and throw hands as usual. A slight massage or rubbing in the direction of the hands of a clock over the abdomen has very good results. A great care should be taken in the direction of the movements of the hands. Rub your hands briskly, when very warm, place one on the abdomen and the other on the back exactly opposite to it. Let your hands be there for 5 or 6 seconds. Repeat this again and again for 3 minutes. Two treatments a day are absolutely necessary. The patient should be given a great deal of fruits. A tumbler of iced water every morning will do immense good. The patient should be made to have good muscular exercise daily.

Give the patient a vapour bath. In addition to this, hot and cold hip baths also if taken alternately for a period of 15 minutes will do immense good to the patient.

CONSUMPTION.

This disease is characterised by excessive pain in the throat accompanied by severe coughing.

Treatment.—Apt suggestions implanted in deep hypnosis only can cure the disease. Passes also should be given from the head down to the knees for 5 minutes. Then apply hot breath over the affected parts.

Free ventilation is absolutely necessary for the patient. This is more or less a contagious disease; and therefore great care should be taken in the treatment. Frequent vapour baths are very useful. For detailed instructions refer to "Lung diseases."

CONVULSIONS.

Put the patient into a deep sleep and apply hot breath over the affected parts of the body and make "passes at contact" over them for 10 or 15 minutes. Give suggestions to counteract the symptoms of the disease. Then awaken the patient.

CRAMP.

This is due to an involuntary contraction of the muscles, either of limbs or the walls of the stomach.

Treatment.—Hot breath application is the most useful thing in such cases. Massage also is necessary. Friction with the warm hand will be very effective. Then adopt proper suggestions.

DEAFNESS.

This more or less comes under Suggestive Therapeutics. Put your patient in deep sleep. Blow hot breath in the ear or ears affected. Give some suggestions to the effect that he is entirely well; he can hear, etc.; then ask him to open his eyes and talk to you. Let your conversation be in a low tone. If he does not hear insist that he can hear you and make him answer you. After a time make him close his eyes and awaken him.

DROPSY.

This is the accumulation of fluid in the limbs under the skin, or in one of the large cavities of the body such as the abdomen or thorax. This accumulation is due to the imperfect circulation through the veins. This disease is generally the outcome of the affections of the heart, liver or kidneys. We can get rid of this sort of accumulation of fluid very successfully by means of "Passes" and "suggestion."

Treatment.—Make the patient sit or lie down on the unaffected side with his eyes closed. Then commence with the "passes at distance" from about 6 inches above the seat of swelling and down to 6 inches below it. Do this for 5 minutes. Apply hot breaths 5 times over the swelling. Then make some "drawing passes" over the affected part and quiver your fingers with nervous energy upon it. Ask him to inhale and exhale breath 3 times. As he opens his eyes, suggest to him "Your swelling will completely subside; you will feel well after each treatment." In all cases of dropsy the administration of a Turkish bath will be of a great service in effecting a cure.

DROWNING.

The treatment for drowning from water is to restore breathing and to promote warmth and circulation by means of massage and hot breath.

Treatment.—Place the patient on his back in a lying posture, with a pillow rolled up underneath the shoulder-blades, and the head hanging back slightly; remove the sand or mud or water, etc., from the mouth of the patient by turning the face over to one side so that the water may run out. Undo all tight clothing from the neck and chest; then try and induce the action of breathing in the following manner: Take hold of his arms by the elbows by standing behind the head of the patient and draw the arms gently and steadily upwards until they meet above the head. Hold the arms up in the same position for 5 seconds and bring the patient's arms and press them firmly against the sides of his chest. Do this steadily and slowly about 12 times a minute until the patient begins to breathe.

Then give a warm bath for 10 minutes. Wrap the patient in warm, dry blankets, massage the limbs under the blankets firmly upwards. Apply bottles filled with warm water to his feet, pit of stomach and under arm pits, etc. When he is in a position to swallow, give some small quantities of warm wine and water or spirit and water or coffee. Allow him to remain in bed and to sleep if possible. If the patient feels a difficulty in breathing, give a hot fomentation on the chest and on back below shoulders.

DYSPEPSIA.

Symptoms.—Pain at the pit of the stomach following food, flatulence, feeling of distention, heart burn, acidity, constipation, alternating with diarrhoea, despondency, disinclination for work, and several other troubles too numerous to be enumerated.

Treatment.—Ask the patient to lie on his back with his eyes closed. Make "passes at contact" from the stomach down over the bowels to the lower part of the body, passing the hands across the front of the hips and then throw hands away. Do this for 5 minutes. Then blow hot breaths over the stomach region 5 times. Make some passes, quivering, over the affected part for 5 minutes. While making passes, "Will" determinedly "All your stomach troubles are leaving you; your pain will be entirely gone; you feel ever so much better." Then ask him to take a long breath and exhale it as quickly as possible. Let him do this 5 times. Then say "When I ask you to open your eyes, all your stomach troubles will be entirely gone; you will feel quite refreshed at each treatment." Ask him to inhale and exhale 3 times and then to open his eyes.

In the same way all kinds of diseases of the bowels and stomach are treated very successfully. The only necessary thing for treating diseases of like nature is to know the place where the disease is situated.

EAR-ACHE AND OTHER EAR TROUBLES.

Treatment—Make your patient, with his eyes closed, lie down so that you can have a look at the affected ear. Cleanse the ear or ears with some warm water with a syringe. Blow hot breath in the ear and make passes around the ear and hold your middle finger at the holes of the ear or ears for about 2 or 3 minutes, and then throw hands away as usual. Then blow hot breath 4 or 5 times over the affected ear or ears. Make some quivering passes for two minutes over the ear and its adjacent parts and throw hands away. When you are doing this, make it a point to "will" determinedly that all his ear troubles will leave him and that he will feel better. Ask the patient to take in a long breath and exhale it quickly. Make him do this 5 times and then open his eyes.

In severe and acute cases where you may not have

time, an application of olive oil into the affected ear will prove very beneficial to the patient.

EMISSIONS—(Nocturnal.)

Treatment.—Put your patient into a deep sleep. Suggest 8 times "You are growing strong; your nerves are getting more energy; you will store great vitality; you will have no emissions in future; your sleep will be undisturbed." Then awaken.

EYE-DISEASES.

Treatment.—Make your patient sit or lie down conveniently in an easy chair. Syringe the eyes well with warm water if there are any foreign bodies in the eyes. Rub the palms together firmly well so as to produce some warmth and quickly lay the palms on the eyes. Remain thus for 2 or 3 minutes. Then apply 5 hot breaths and stroke the eyelids gently with the tips of your fingers for some time and this will be beneficial. Any kind of rubbing over the eyes should always be from the outer edge towards the nose. A bathing with cold water, that has been kept in the open air, the night previous, is most useful.

Blindness also can be treated in this way, but it is better to put the patient into Hypnosis and then give positive suggestions to the effect that his sight is improving, that he will see better when awakened, etc. The whole effect lies in the way in which the suggestions are imparted.

FEVERS.

These may be classed as Putrid, Malignant, Bilious, Gastric and Intermittent.

Magnetism very soon assuages a fever or at least its paroxysms. It puts a stop to the delirium; it imparts strength at the same time, when it diminishes the agi-

tation of the nerves. But sometimes the violence of
the fever may thwart the magnetic action at first, but its
continued application will gain mastery over it.

It is the surest agent in cures of putrid and malignant fevers. In the former it sustains strength, and in
the latter it regulates the motion.

In nervous fevers Magnetism soothes the nerves and
restores equilibrium. In bilious and gastric fevers Magnetism gives strength and vitality to the stomach and
produces evacuation.

Of all kinds of fevers the intermittent fever requires
a good deal of caution, judgment and perseverance.
You should treat such patients at the very moment of
attack. Generally, fevers cease after 5 or 6 successive
treatments. It is also good to continue the treatment
for some more days and give the patient magnetised
water to drink. This will greatly prevent the return
of the complaint.

Treatment.—Ask the patient to lie on his back and
close his eyes. Make passes at distance from the crown
of the patient's head down over the region of the heart
and thence to the feet. Throw hands at the end of each
pass. At each pass "will" determinedly that his fever
will cease; and give passes for 15 minutes. While giving passes you may feel a slight burning sensation in
the tips of your fingers as well as in the hollow of the
palm. In such cases dip the hand into water acidulated
with vinegar and continue passes. By such an act you
may soothe paroxysm and often produce perspiration,
which is a sure sign of the cessation of the fever.

Then ask him to inhale and exhale as usual, thrice.
Then say in a positive tone "Open your eyes, you are
all right; your fever is competely gone; you feel a decided relief."

There is another method of treatment for fevers which
is very effective, when all resources fail. The Turkish
bath is the most efficacious method in eradicating the
poisonous effects of morbid fevers, Ague, Malaria, etc.

FLATULENCE.

This is more or less another form of Dyspepsia and should therefore be treated as Dyspepsia.

GOUT.

This is a very bad disease and can be cured effectively only by Magnetic healing. This first attacks the smaller joints as the toes and fingers and generally the people affected are indolent and luxurious. This is a disease of the advanced life. At times this may combine with Rheumatism.

Treatment.—The parts inflamed should be well wrapped in Magnetised Cotton and many "passes at distance" made over the affected parts for a period of 10 minutes. Hot breath and friction of the hands should be next applied followed by a thorough massage. A continuous treatment will cure any form of gout. This may attack the other parts of the body also. It should be borne in mind that sufficient warmth alone will keep the patient in a good condition.

GRAVEL.

Gravel, or a deposit in the urine may be passed through the kidneys in large quantities in the form of powder, grit, sand or small stones. When the deposit is fine, it causes very little pain, but when the fragments become large, an inexorable pain is created and at times affects the bladder; when it will have to be removed by operation.

Treatment.—The patient should be made to sit in a chair and a hot bath given daily for some days. A copious supply of mineral water or barley water or linseed water or weak tea is also better. A strict vegetable diet is preferable in such cases.

HEADACHE.

Treatment.—Note the location of the pain in the patient. Request him to sit in a chair with his eyes closed. Stand behind him and allow his head to rest against your front. Make "passes at contact" with both hands commencing from the centre of his forehead and passing around the head as far as possible above the ears. Throw your hands away at the end of each pass. Do this for 3 or 4 minutes. Then place your left hand at the back part of his head and your right upon his forehead. Now exert strong pressure with both of your hands for 45 seconds; similarly apply lateral pressure on the head for 45 seconds. At this stand in front of the patient and make a dozen quick downward short local passes at distance with both hands, from the crown of the patient's head down over the temples and thence to the cheek bones. After doing this tell the patient to take in a long deep breath by the nostrils and to exhale it through the mouth as quickly as possible. Let him do this 5 times. Be sure to make the above said passes at each act of exhaling. Then say in a positive tone: "Open your eyes, you are all right; your headache is completely gone; you feel better now."

Remember during the whole treatment you should determinedly "will" that he will feel better after your treatment, and that he will be completely relieved of his headache. Generally one treatment will suffice to cure even the very bad headache. If you do not succeed in your first attempt another treatment can be given immediately.

In very severe cases of headaches such as those resulting from Dyspepsia and several similar causes, the best course to adopt is to give your patient a vapour bath accompanied by the ordinary mode of treatment as above.

To cure the headache, attended with cold feet, put your palms on the patient's head for several minutes, continue the long passes and repeat passes over the limbs. The feet will turn warm and the head clear.

HEART DISEASE.

This is a serious complaint. Only experienced operators can undertake the treatment.

Treatment.—Make your patient sit or lie down in a convenient position. Then make a few "passes at distance" over the region of the heart. The passes should be made for 15 minutes by the right hand. Passes in half circles are sufficient. At the end of each pass, as usual, you should throw away your hands. Blow the hot breath 5 times over the region of the heart. Then make quivering passes for 5 minutes and suggest "Your heart troubles will entirely cease; you will feel better after each treatment: you will positively be relieved of your heart troubles." Then ask him to take a deep breath and exhale it quickly. Let him do this 3 times. During the whole treatment the patient should have his eyes closed.

HEART BURN.

Treat this disease as above. A few passes over the portion affected is sufficient. A little soda with fresh milk taken every morning will have a salutory effect.

HIC-COUGH.

Treatment.—Ask the patient to lie down with his eyes closed. Make a few "passes at distance" over the throat and give the patient a very small piece of ice to be swallowed. Ask the patient to inhale the air by the nostrils, and keep it for a short time in the lungs and then expel by the mouth. Let him do this for 5 times. A thorough massage around the sides of the body with a little pressure on the stomach will be very useful. A little firm pressing near the end of the Collar bones next to the throat with the thumb will also be very effective.

HYDROPHOBIA.

This is a very fatal disease, which arises from the bite of a rabid cat, dog or other animal.

A magnetised bandage of wool should be put over the bite if it is on the arm or the leg, and suggestions in deep hypnosis alone will cure it. The patient should be cheered up as far as possible.

HYPOCHONDRIASIS.

This may develop into Melancholia if not arrested in the growth. No medicine can do any good. Proper suggestions as "You will not feel nervous; you are happy and cheerful; you are strong and well; you have perfect mastery over you; when awakened, you will be all right, etc., should be given in deep hypnosis. Then blow hot breaths over the heart a few times and awaken him after suggesting that he will feel well, etc.

HYSTERIA.

This complaint occurs most frequently in young women who have been overworked or whose general health is very poor. The attack comes on quite suddenly. The countenance is generally distorted; eyelids or eyeballs are quivering; and a great difficulty is felt in taking a deep breath. Hysteria occurs in many forms, but the above are the most common forms that are met with. It should be carefully treated, as it is a very dangerous disease. It cannot be cured by Magnetic Healing; if at all any cure can be effected it should be done by Suggestive Therapeutics alone. Only experienced men can undertake this.

Treatment.—During the attack the dress should be entirely loosened; a thorough ventilation should be allowed and even sprinkling with cold water is beneficial. The extremeties should be well rubbed. A sudden throwing of a bucketful of cold water over the head and chest will work like a miracle. Such people should always have cold baths.

When there is no attack, put the patient into a deep sleep and suggest "When I awaken you, you will be perfectly well; you will not be nervous; you will feel well in every way; you will have perfect control over yourself; you will feel strong." Then blow hot breath over the region of the heart, 4 or 5 times and suggest in a positive tone, "Now when I awaken you all this nervousness will be gone; you will be entirely well." Then after a time awaken the patient.

HYDROCELE.

This is a collection of bad water in the bag encircling the testicles. A slight tapping over the part will give a temporary relief.

INFLUENZA.

This is an epidemic disorder. The symptoms are, depression, chillness, running from the eyes and nose, headache, cough, restlessness and fever.

Keep the patient in bed, in a cool ventilated room, but free from all kinds of draughts. A good nourishment must be given. Use suggestions freely. If rheumatism sets in treat accordingly.

INSOMNIA OR SLEEPLESSNESS.

This arises from a variety of causes. It may be due to pain, restlessness or excessive activity of the brain.

Treatment.—Put the patient into a deep sleep. Make "passes at contact" over the region of the heart and over the abdomen for a period of 15 minutes; then suggest in a positive tone, "You will not be nervous; you will sleep well; you will not be restless; you will feel well and have a sound sleep; you will go to bed at 8 p. m. and rise at 6 a. m. Repeat the above suggestions 10 times and tell him after a while, "when I awaken you, you will feel well." Then awaken the patient as usual after having given him ample time.

LEPROSY.

Though not an infectious, yet it is a contagious disease. Unless you have no repugnant feelings at the sight of lepers you should not undertake the treatment of the disease. Vapour baths should be given. Before boiling the water, magnetise it and it would be better if you also put some "muriate of calcium" in it. Cleanliness should be strictly observed. When you magnettise water for such cases, wash your hands with soap and water. An occasional use of horsegrain as die will be very beneficial.

LUMBAGO.

This is a form of rheumatism which effects the muscles of the back and loins. It is usually due to cold, and often persists for many weeks or even months, unless steps are taken to effect a cure. The pain is usually very severe, especially when the patient attempts to stoop down.

For treatment, refer to rheumatism.

LUNG DISEASES.

The chief diseases of the lungs are, Consumption, Bronchitis, Pneumonia and Pleurisy. All these are generally accompanied by cough, expectoration, loss of flesh and pain in the sides. Sometimes these are attended by even spitting of blood. Night sweating is also one of the chief characteristics. All these are treated in a same way.

Treatment.—Ask your patient to lie on his back in a convenient posture and ask him to close his eyes. Make "passes at contact" with both your hands, starting a

little above the upper portion of the chest of the patient
down to the lower one. At this let your right hand
cross over the patient's left side and your left to his
right. Then throw your hands away. Repeat for 15
minutes. Apply hot breath 5 or 6 times over the whole
region of the chest. Suggest to the patient, "Your pain
has gone; you feel better; there is nothing the matter
with you." Ask him to breathe as usual.

MUMP.

This is an infectious disorder resulting in the inflammation of a gland behind the jaw and in front and
below the ear. A good vapour bath is sufficient. It
would be advantageous if passes are given over the
affected parts. Apply hot breath. As usual make the
patient inhale and exhale breath thrice. When he is
breathing, make quivering passes and throw hands.

NERVOUS DEBILITY.

Treatment.—Put your patient in a deep sleep. Make
passes at distance from the base of the brain down to
the small of the back. Do this for 15 minutes. Blow
5 hot breaths over the region of the heart and suggest
very positively, "When I awaken you, all your nervousness will completely disappear; you will feel a decided
relief in your body; there will be nothing the matter
with you; your nerves will feel strong; you will be
perfectly relieved in every way." Then awaken him.

NEURALGIA.

It is otherwise called "nerve pain," which may occur
in any part of the body, but the commonest variety is
that which attacks the face. The pain is usually very
intense and may keep the patient awake for many nights
in succession. When the pain attacks the arm it is
generally known as *ulnar neuralgia*, whilst the same
pain attacking the sciatic nerve of the leg is known as

Sciatica. Much may be accomplished by timely care and attention to ward off Neuralgia of any kind.

Treatment.—Seat the patient in a chair if the seat of the pain is in face or make him lie down upon the unaffected side, if affected in the arms or legs. Tell him to close his eyes. Rub your hands well and warm; lay both your hands on the affected parts and hold them there for 2 minutes. Then blow 5 hot breaths in both ears of the patient and also over the affected parts. Then make "passes at distance" from the crown of the patient's head down to the jaw bone for 10 minutes and throw hands at the end of each pass. While giving passes "will" determinedly that his pain will be gone and that he will be very much relieved after each treatment. Then ask him to exhale and inhale 5 breaths in succession. While he exhales speak to him positively, "Open your eyes; all your pain is gone; you feel quite refreshed."

Strict attention to the following should be adhered to: Diet, regular and homely exercise and sufficient amount of sleep, and the avoidance of badly ventilated rooms. Turkish bath is very effectual in the treatment of this disease.

PAIN.

All sorts of pain, wherever situated, can best be relieved by the application of massage, hot breath and suggestions.

PARALYSIS.

There are many kinds of Paralysis and all arise out of the nervous complications. It is a disease produced by the failure of the proper nerves to carry intelligence from the brain to any particular muscle or organ, and the gradual disuse of the muscle or organ owing to the lack of communication, becomes too stiffened to act. In such cases the proper treatment should be to restore a normal activity to the affected nerves and re-establish communication with the muscles.

Application of magnetism together with massage and vapour bath is the sure means to cure all kinds of Paralysis. It restores sensibility and reëstablishes the movements.

Treatment.—Make the patient lie on his face in a convenient posture. Slap his spinal cord as hard as the patient can bear, from top to bottom, for about 10 minutes, and also rub the spine with your hands until you find a ruddy glow all over. Make "passes at contact" from the neck down over the spine to the small of the back for about 5 minutes. Then massage the affected limbs. Let this occupy 5 minutes. Ask the patient to turn; give quick drawing and quivering passes for 2 minutes from the top of the head to the toe. Then apply hot breath over the affected parts, at the back of the brain, small of the back and over the heart. Hot breaths should be blown 4 times in each place. Then ask the patient to close his eyes and take 5 long deep breaths and exhale them as quickly as possible one after another. Now suggest, "Open your eyes, you are perfectly well." At the close of the treatment rub the affected parts with a few drops of Alcohol.

If the patient is affected in his legs, ask him to stand up and walk. Heed not to the words of the patient; help him to walk a little every day. Every affected part should be made to be used a little. Frequent exercise of the muscles is absolutely necessary together with the administration of vapour baths.

Suggestive Therapeutics Treatment.—Put the patient in deep sleep and suggest, "When I count ten, you will be perfectly well; your paralysis will have disappeared; there will be nothing the matter with you." Then count up to ten and as you say "ten," suggest in a very positive tone, "Now you are all right."

Make him move his limbs as above and at the close of the treatment before awakening, suggest, "When you awaken, you will continue to walk; you will have no difficulty." Then awaken the patient. The Treatment should be given until he is alright.

PALSY OR WRITERS' CRAMP.

A thorough shampooing of the affected part and suggestions in Hypnosis will produce marvellous results.

PILES.

The best Method of treatment is to administer magnetised cold water bath over the affected part of the body. The cold water should have been kept in open air the night previous. Diet should be fully regulated. All kinds of stimulants should be avoided. Specially ripened vegetables should as far as possible b discontinued.

RHEUMATISM.

This may be classed under two heads: Acute and Chronic.

Acute and Its Symptoms.—Pain in the joints, attended with fever; profuse sweating and general weakness of the body.

Chronic and Its Symptoms.—Severe pain in the knees, ankles, hips, shoulders and arms. Exposure either to wet or cold will subject the patient to worst pains. Thickening of the joints of the arms, knees, ankles and shoulders is frequently the result of this state of rheumatism of the system. There is congestion of the throat, which is also the result of the above state of Rheumatism.

Treatment.—First localise the pain in the body Have the patient, with his eyes closed, seated in a chair, or if convenient, lie down in a comfortable position upon the unaffected part. Then "make passes at distance" over the affected part for about 10 minutes. Then massage the affected parts for 5 minutes. Apply hot breath 4 or 5 times over the seat of pain. Then make some drawing passes over it and throw hands away. Do this for 2 minutes. At this ask him to inhale and exhale breath 5 times. Make him open his eyes and suggest in a positive tone: "All your pain has gone; you are completely free from Rheumatism; you have perfect strength in your body; you can freely move and walk; there is absolutely nothing the matter with you; you are alright."

At the close of treatment make it a point to give a Turkish bath to your patient. Great remedial quick results will follow if you put some "Extract of Pumilio Pine" into the water before boiling it. The vapour bath should occupy at the most 15 minutes.

Before giving your vapour baths, dissolve a handful of common salt in 4 ounces of water (magnetised previously) and rub this solution of salt water over the affected parts. Allow the patient to remain still for 5 minutes until the salt application dries.

RICKETS.

This is owing to an imperfect development of the bones. These are characterised by deformities of the limbs, of the pelvis, of the spine, of the ribs, and in many instances of the bones of the skull. These are visible generally in children at birth or a little later. The child should always be given a salt water bath and if pain exists magnetised salt water sponging will give immediate relief. The child should be kept from walking as far as possible. A thorough massage with the constant application of hot breath over the affected part is indispensable.

SCORPION STING.

Ask the patient to close his eyes. Make passes at distance for 5 minutes commencing about 6 inches from above the seat of pain and drawing down to 6 inches below it. Throw hands away at each pass. Blow hot breath over the seat of pain 4 or 5 times. Then rub your hands briskly well and warm and quickly apply the palm over the seat of pain and remain thus for 15 seconds. Do this for 3 minutes. Then make some quivering passes over the seat of pain and throw hands at each pass. Do this for 2 minutes. Then suggest in a positive tone, "When I tell you to open your eyes, you will find that your pain is entirely gone; you will feel quite relieved; you will be alright." Then ask him to open his eyes.

In the same way all sorts of pain in the body wherever it may be situated, can be relieved very successfully.

SCROFULA, SYPHILIS, ETC.

These are contagious and dangerous blood diseases which human beings are subject to.

Symptoms.—Production of hard humorous ulcers and abscesses and gradual decay of the bone substance of the body. The patients affected by these have generally great mental anxiety and physical torment.

Treatment.—The only efficacious method of treating these, is to give the patient a vapour bath daily till the symptoms of the disease gradually wear away.

The bath application is the only best and effective mode of rooting out this dangerous disease successfully.

A week's treatment, will show miraculous good effects even in the most obstinate and helpless cases of the above, as well as in Gonorrhœa, Gleet, Incontinence of urine, Irritation, Inflammation, Ulceration of the bladder or kidneys and also in several other blood diseases.

STAMMERING.

Treatment.—Put the patient into a deep sleep and suggest "You will not stammer again; you can talk as well as any body; there is nothing the matter with you."

Then ask him to open his eyes and make him read some pages from a book, making him to repeat several times the words which he is not able to say well in his normal state. As he is in Hypnosis he will read as well as anybody. Then let him close his eyes. Then suggest, "You will always read and talk well; you will have no difficulty in talking in future; you will continue to read and talk as you did now." Then awaken him. The treatment may occupy half an hour. The patient must be made to read and talk under Hypnosis. No deep sleep is necessary.

SUN STROKE.

It is a congestion of the brain resulting from the heat of the sun. For such diseases, great care should be taken to evacuate the bowels daily and to shelter the head from the action of the sun by suitable head-gear. Cold baths and out-door exercises in the early morning are greatly recommended for the prevention of an attack. Care should also be taken to provide the patient with flannel clothing and covering for the head, made of a material devoid of colour, so that the sun's rays may be reflected, instead of being absorbed. The treatment consists in having the bowels thoroughly evacuated and also to apply ice to the head at the same time.

TOOTH ACHE.

Ask the patient to sit in a chair with his eyes closed. Make "passes at distance" over the affected parts for 10 minutes, commencing from 6 inches above the seat of pain down over the affected part and thence a little farther. Apply hot breath over the seat of pain for 4 or 5 times. Then make quivering passes over the part affected and throw hands at each pass. Then suggest in a positive tone, "Your toothache is entirely gone; you will feel quite refreshed after this treatment; you are alright, open your eyes."

WOMB TROUBLES.

All kinds of troubles existing in the womb can be treated as follows:

Make the patient lie on her back with her eyes closed. Make "passes at distance" with both hands, commencing at the pit of the stomach and going down over abdomen to the lower part of the body, and throw hands away. Let this take 10 minutes. Blow hot breath over the region of womb 5 times. Then place your hands palms down over the abdomen (directly over the flesh is preferred) and suggest, "All your womb troubles are leaving you; you will feel a decided relief all over that part; you will feel quite refreshed after each treatment." Then ask her to inhale and exhale 4 times and to open her eyes.

Generally 2 or 3 treatments will entirely remove the pain.

In the cases of excessive flooding, falling of the womb, etc., make upward passes at contact with both hands with some slight pressure, from the lower regions of the womb to the pit of the stomach. Shake hands at each pass. While making such passes "will" determinedly that in future the flow of blood will entirely stop, that she will feel strong and quite refreshed

Here, friction of the hands applied to the seat of the disease, will do a great deal of relief.

Instruct your patient not to undergo very hard exercise at any time, before she is entirely cured.

As a caution to the practitioner of Magnetic Healing we wish to instruct you not to take any advantage of the confidence the patient has placed in your integrity, honesty and purity of thought. Be a gentleman in all your acts while you are treating a patient. Have purity at heart if you wish to effect wonders.

CHAPTER III.

HOW TO GENERATE MAGNETISM FROM NATURE.

We now give you an exercise, which if you follow in all candour will tremendously store in you magnetism or nerve force. This will stand you in good need, as at every treatment you are apt to be drained and weakened by a flow of the fluid from you to the patient. You can actually feel this new force tingling in your veins even after the short practice of a week.

EXERCISE.

Stand erect with your hands hanging loosely at your sides. Close your eyes. Relax all muscles of your body. Fill your lungs fully with fresh air by inhaling through the nostrils. Keep adding still more fresh air by mouth, until you can fill your lungs as fully as possible. Remain thus for 3 or 4 seconds. Then exhale through the mouth all the air particles in the lungs very slowly; and remain still without exhaling or inhaling for 10 seconds. Repeat process and continue for 15 minutes. During the whole process of inhaling and exhaling, repeat mentally with all positiveness, "I draw a good deal of magnetism from Nature; I consciously absorb this force and it is under my possession and control."

This exercise should be practised in the open air every morning and evening.

(180)

DEVELOPMENT OF THE WILL.

We live in deeds, not years: in thoughts, not breaths;
  In feelings, not in figures on a dial.
We should count time by heart-throbs. He most lives
  Who thinks most, feels the noblest, acts the best.

Bailey: "Human Life."

Human life beset with many obstacles and vicissitudes is like a ship which is about to quit the safe and quiet harbour in which it was safe, to launch on the dark and unknown ocean, where so many a gallant vessel has gone down before. Young men, like young Commander of the ships, have to steer their course through this vast ocean. How much would the disquietude be increased when the Commander has thrown away the very chart and compass by which he was prepared to guide the ship through the doubtful perils of the voyages! So is the case with now-a-days young men, who do not care to cultivate their mental powers and guard against the overwhelming dangers of the world.

Dear Reader! for the cultivation of that, which leads to that desired termination—the safe and successful career—of our life work, we hereunder give you the charts. It is only when you master them, you will be able to master thyself.

THE PHILOSOPHY OF THE HUMAN MIND.

"Mind is the master-power that moulds and makes,
And man is mind, and ever more he takes
And tool of thought, and, shaping what he wills,
Brings forth a thousand joys, a thousand ills:—
He thinks in secret, and it comes to pass;
Environment is but his looking glass."

James Allen.

Man advances from the lower to the higher; from the bottom to the top of the head, from the lower to the higher strata of the brain, and from the soul to the spirit, and from this mundane world to the heaven above. The higher part in nature is most important and impenetrable to the lay mind.

Man commences life in the mineral world of existence and advances till the very presence of the Almighty Lord is reached. And this rising depends on his thoughts and actions. From birth until death the body is maturing the Soul and that is becoming and eternalising the spirit. The time, ways and methods for such an attainment and evolution is while you are in this physical body. Take heed ere it be too late.

All thought is concentrated in the Corpus Callosum, which is the point to which all the exterior brain fibres converge and bring the brain and its product-mind, into one great centre. All concentrated thought continually vibrates and forms into stronger mind elements by developing the nervous matter it uses and all such development arises by constant exercise. The mind can be cultivated by exercise which will in turn develop the brain.

Hence you build your own destiny—eternal—by pursuing a particular line of thought, as is wisely said, "All that we wish may be obtained by knowing how to think."

The All Wise Creator has not given this extraordinary ability to a selected few. This is only a cultivation of the power which is latent in one and all. The simple culture of that will put you in position "how to think." By so thinking you can exchange your surroundings and bring to you whatever your heart desires. You can alleviate your sufferings, depressions and pains. What we now teach you here, is, simply the way of thinking.

THE WILL AND ITS POWER.

Will is the grand culmination of the complex mental faculties of man. The act of *willing* expresses a fixed determination of the mind. It is an important feature in the development of Personal Magnetism. It is the

power that sets the forces of mind to work and it is
this that directs them along a definite line. The will
is said to be of two kinds, the strong and the weak.
A strong will is a mental force, ever on the alert and
ever active. It is with this, people are controlled and
nations are ruled.

A strong-willed man is he by whose mere presence
people are awed and stricken terror in their minds. He
need not speak or need utter a sound even. There is
something in him which goes to make people revere
him. He keeps his mind always tense and his will is
more and more strengthened. He knows no failure. He
cannot fail for he creates resources then and there and
ever forges ahead toward his goal. All desires that lie
within range of human possibilities can be accomplished
by him only if he wills in that direction. The single-
ness and straightforwardness of his thought and confidence in his ability are the keys with which he unlocks
the doors of success. He does not turn his attention
to every new thing that occurs; but he pursues a definite course and thus prevents his energies from flowing
in many directions and being wasted. He makes use
of everything that comes in his way. He does not neglect even trifles and never engages in anything that
does not pertain to his goal. There is no trial which
is too great for him. No task too severe. An indomitable will carries him ever onward and onward. He
delights in difficulties because they afford him an opportunity to test his ability, if at all he encounters any
at times, they spur him on and on to greater efforts.
His heart and soul are in the work he undertakes, and
what would seem a burden to others becomes a pleasure
to him. His sole aim is improvement. He seeks oppor-
tunities, and employs every moment and finds happiness
in contemplating over them.

If you desire to be such a man, it is within your
grasp. Exercise your mind in order to develop your
will, as the will can be developed and strengthened just
as any other member or part of the body. Constant

use strengthens and increases the will power. Now use on the other hand emaciates and weakens it. It is worth more to you than anything else. It gives you power over people, it gives you influence, it brings you happiness and it creates in you health and wealth.

You know these things just as we know. You can positively develop your will. Be magnetic and you can have a wonderful force of character. No matter how deficient you may be, if you but follow implicitly our instructions, do just as we tell you and continue to work at it daily with unflinching perseverance, you will eventually attain success little short of miracles.

In developing your will, you will have to use a combined process of auto-suggestions and auto-hypnosis. You know already what amount of good you have derived from your instructions. You can develop greater courage, stronger will power, energy, persistency, concentration, self-confidence, self-control, strong memory, etc. Not only these, bad habits, nervous fears, acute worry, anger, grief, hate, stage fright, etc., can be eliminated and set aside at will. All these things mean success and more than success; they mean happiness.

LESSON I.

We now give you some psycho-physical exercises which if you follow in all candour, we are sure they will develop your will power to a marvelous extent. The exercises will seem to you to be innocent in themselves; but if you practice them properly the results that accrue will be beneficial from the very start. To use them intelligently means success to you, because they develop new characteristics which go to make up a success of you. You will notice their effect upon yourself, at the first opportunity you use them. For instance, if you take up the first exercise for developing stronger will power, the chances are, that even after the first experiment you will feel more energetic, more determined and more enthusiastic. By this we do not say, that it is possible to develop your will all in a minute. But con-

tinued practice of these exercises twice or thrice a day
for 30 minutes or more, in the privacy of your room,
makes the change for good in you stronger and more
lasting every day.   It is a great mistake often committed by some of our students that as soon as they feel
a change in themselves on the first day, they are so
very delighted and enthusiastic over their first results
that they try to do too much, that is, they seek to
acquire several new characteristics all at once in a day.
It is a mistake of course for it scatters their mental
forces in different channels simultaneously and the consequence is they are not a bit perfectly developed in
any.   If you wish to attain perfection what you will
have to do is to take up the first exercise and stick to
it and continue the same for a long time even though
you feel to have attained a strong and powerful will
power.   What we ask you to do is to get a strong hold
of it so that it may be a deep rooted one in you.   Then
take the others in turn, one by one and not in close
succession; but separately at leisure, as you know that
"too many cooks spoil the broth."   When you have cultivated all these you will feel proud of yourself and of
the wonders you can do.

Before undertaking to do anything we shall teach you
the means of hypnotising yourself.

AUTO-HYPNOSIS.

Retire into a quiet room; lie or sit in a convenient
position.   Relax all your muscles perfectly.   Look intently at the root of your nose.   In a short time you
will fall into deep hypnosis.

EXERCISE I.

Retire into a quiet room.   Write the 3 suggestions
given below in a bold hand on 3 separate sheets of
white paper.   Take the paper with first suggestion and
place it before you on a table.   Seat yourself, relaxing
your muscles, on an easy chair and gaze at the tip of

nose so that your eyes may be 3 feet from the paper without any winking whatever, repeating the suggestion in the paper over and over mentally, with all the energy, the fire and determination of your whole nature. Commence to breathe in through your *nostrils* as much pure air as possible, slowly, while you gaze at tip of nose. Allow the inhaled air to remain in the lungs as long as you can. Then exhale through your *mouth* in a slow rhythmic way all the air you inhaled. Stop a few seconds and then repeat process of inhaling and exhaling, gazing at tip of nose, repeating over and over the suggestion mentally with all positiveness. You may within a short time, feel drowsy, and your eyes may begin to droop, but keep repeating the suggestion mentally as long as you are awake. This exercise should be continued for a period of 30 minutes or more if necessary and it will be better if you practice this just at the early morning, mid-day, evening and just when you go to bed at night. Similarly take the 2nd suggestion on the 2nd day and the other on the 3rd. When you have finished the 3 suggestions, take the 3 together and repeat them as in the aforesaid process for 12 more days.

SUGGESTIONS FOR DEVELOPING WILL POWER.

I. My will is strong; nobody can resist a strong will; I have a strong will.

II. I am a power; I admit no limitations; things must go as I will.

III. I claim all from infinite substance; I demand and all things come to me at my will, for I have an indomitable will.

LESSON II.

We now give you some auto-suggestions to develop to a great extent your Personal Magnetism and several others for your self culture. No doubt you have already developed to some extent this mysterious power, but to create in you a stronger personality the following lessons are given here. Practice these exercises as thoroughly as possible and they will surely develop in you a very strong personality.

PERSONAL MAGNETISM.

To have a good strong and magnetic personality, your first step should be to care for your *health*. For, a healthy physique is requisite for attaining success in any undertaking. The amount of work you can do mainly depends upon the health and vigour of your nerves and brains. So a thorough nourishment of them is very desirable.

A regular early morning cold water bath, accompanied by the practice of these exercises, will positively develop a health aura in you. Always be temperate in everything and avoid all excesses. Always endeavour to strike at the root of disease by providing clean, wholesome and beautiful surroundings. Select always the most simple, yet refined and nourishing vegetable foods available. Have some recreation; for it is absolutely necessary for your bodily as well as your mental vigour. Have sufficient sleep at night to give rest both to your body as well as to your mind. Go through the deep breathing exercises daily, every morning, mid-day, evening and even at night when you retire to bed. In short, the rules of diet, the habit of deep breathing, the wearing of proper clothing that does not in any way impede the free passage of pure air over the body, the habit of bathing in cold water in the early morning, free use of water, regular rest, proper amount of recreation together with a sufficient amount of muscular exercise—are essential for the up keep of your health.

SUGGESTIONS TO IMPROVE HEALTH.

I. "I keep a sound health; I am healthy."
II. "I have a great store of vitality and nerve force." "I am perfectfully healthy."

III.   "No sickness with me; I am in sound health
Practice these suggestions as in Exercise I and
will develop your health aura.

To be successful in all your undertakings you sho
have unbounded confidence in yourself. This does
mean egotism but absolute self control. You sho
always be modest, calm, cool and self possessed. Wl
ever any danger is at hand, if somebody about yo
frightened, if failure is your lot, or if a person se
a quarrel with you, in all these cases, you should ne
get excited. Do not worry concerning your future. `
should bear in mind that worry is full of life destr
ing influence. All mental scientists are of opinion
there is nothing that destroys the brain cells so rap
as worry. Worry is said to kill life, heart and m
netism.

LESSON III.

We are now going to tell you something about
culture. In self culture character comes forem
Character is the true distinction between man and be
It brings real happiness, esteem, peace of mind
inner satisfaction. All leaders and great successful r
owed their success to some points of moral excelle
in their character. A man of some force of chara
has self-esteem, self-knowledge and self-control, and
these are the 3 essentials which go to make one's
a sovereign power. Upon this understanding, in
formation of character you should assign the forem
place to the development of will and the control of y
thoughts and desires. "Guard thy thoughts well
thoughts are heard in Heaven," is a golden max
The right control of thoughts and desires promotes y
present as well as your future life. Therefore educ
your mind and will thoroughly and follow the dicta
of your conscience—the ruler of heart. Strengthen y
moral fibre, by the practice of truthfulness, kindn
firmness, fearlessness, independence and countenar

Practice these virtues in your daily life and make these part and parcel of yourself. To be still more plain, be a bold adherent of truth and thus establish a reputation for being truthful, enabling others to rely on your words with perfect surety. Be kind and compassionate and forgiving. It has been the conduct of the great heroic souls to shed tears of pity at the sad plight of others, and if sufficiently strong to exert themselves to the utmost to work out their deliverance; to take pride in doing acts of mercy and in assisting frail humanity out of misery and trouble brought on by its own weakness and recklessness. Such awe inspiring precepts of high mindedness and generosity shalt thou follow in thy life. Be open and pure hearted. Conquer vice. Resoluteness and independence should be the predominant features of every action of yours. Lastly but not leastly, be a friend and lover of all; try to purge out vices from others and lead them into the noble path of virtue and inculcate in them a knowledge of virtues and their foundation, virtues regarding oneself, virtues and vices in relation to superior, equal and inferiors and their reaction upon each other.

LESSON IV.

EXERCISE II.

We give you several sets of suggestions, to be practiced as in Exercise I to develop your character, self-control, success and happiness thoughts, etc.

SUGGESTIONS TO WARD OFF ANGER.

I. "I am determined not to get angry with any."
II. "I shall control my temper at all times."
III. "I have complete control over my anger."

LESSON V.

EXERCISE III.

SUGGESTIONS FOR FEARLESSNESS.

I. "I am fearless; I will not fear at any time."
II. "I am a part of the Divine Self; Nobody shall hurt me; therefore there is no fear from any."
III. "I shall not fear; I am completely at home always."

LESSON VI.

EXERCISE IV.

SUGGESTIONS FOR SUCCESS.

I. "I am made of success; I am made for success; my goal is success."
II. "All success. There is no failure with me."
III. "I will have perfect success in all my undertakings; I know no failure; I cannot fail; I shall succeed; I will succeed."

LESSON VII.

EXERCISE V.

SUGGESTIONS FOR HAPPINESS.

I. "I am all joy; no anxiety can touch me and I have no worry."
II. "All is harmony; intense harmony."
III. "I am radiating happiness; I am content; all is mine; I am happiness itself."

LESSON VIII.

EXERCISE VI.

SUGGESTIONS FOR AVOIDING WORRY OF MIND.

I. "Nothing shall worry me."
II. "I will not allow myself to worry over anything."
III. "I am determined not to worry; there is no worry with me; I am all right."

LESSON IX.

EXERCISE VII.

SUGGESTIONS FOR DEVELOPING PERSONAL INFLUENCE.

I. "I am a magnet; none can withstand my attraction."
II. "No one can repel my influence; I will sway over all."
III. "My will is law."

CHAPTER IV.

SPIRITUAL CLAIRVOYANCE

Clairvoyance is clear mental vision. It is a psychological condition of the mind in which the soul has the power to see or understand the thought and psychic conditions and objects beyond the range of physical vision. This soul-sight increases in its lucidity as we retard the physical activities below the normal state.

Clairvoyance is not a common possession. It is a most valuable psychic possession for man. Except a few spiritually cultured noble souls the general populace do not appreciate this psychic power. This mysterious power is not the sole possession of a gifted few, but all are endowed with the faculty. It lies latent in all. It only rests with them to develop it. This spiritual faculty of man can be cultivated just as any other faculty. In some, this develops in a very short time, and in others it takes a pretty long time. This depends mainly upon their temperaments and character. The leading scientists of the day have been already convinced about the existence of such a power.

The resultant benefits of this wonderful power are manifold. Humanity can be learnt thoroughly to some extent; the future destiny of one can be made known; all diseases and ailments known to man can be diagnosed and the best remedial advice can be had in connection therewith. It may also be used to find out lost or stolen property and may even be used to ferret out murders, etc. And lastly it is the key to investigate the

(192)

mysteries of nature and also the divine path of soul perfection.

We teach you here how to develop the spiritual faculty, and if you diligently work at these lessons you will be amply repaid for your time and perseverance. For convenience sake, we divide clairvoyance into three realms.

I.   Mediumistic Clairvoyance.
II. Intent Clairvoyance.
III. Psychic Clairvoyance.

Mediumistic clairvoyance is the development of that august power—Clairvoyance—in a sensitive or subject by means of mesmeric passes "at distance."

The Intent and Psychic Clairvoyances offer very favourable conditions in the normal state for the development of this faculty upon yourself.   All the three processes mainly lead to the same goal and the methods employed are simply to aid you in subduing the sense activities and thereby offering a favourable condition for the mastery of the psychic powers over the mind as the sub-conscious mind is naturally invested with these powers and many more that have not come to light as yet.

I. MEDIUMISTIC CLAIRVOYANCE.
WHOM TO EMPLOY AS SUBJECTS FOR MEDIUMISTIC CLAIRVOYANCE.

From long practical experience we give you some hints how to find out suitable subjects for the practice of mediumistic clairvoyance.   Healthy, intelligent and fair looking persons of either sex, between the ages of 14 and 30, make the best subjects for experiment and research.

HOW TO CULTIVATE MEDIUMISTIC CLAIRVOYANCE.

Select a subject, make him lie down on a couch or sofa in a room void of all disturbance and noise.   Absolute silence should reign in the room. The slightest noise or disturbance will cause great danger. Stand by his side, ask him to close his eyes and to relax his body and mind. Make passes at distance, commencing from the crown of the head with the fingers of your hands slightly curved, slowly down over the chin and thence to the region of heart. This should take one minute. Then continue down and make one circular pass over the region of heart for a period of 45 seconds, and thence down to the pit of the stomach; now diverge your hands and make passes down the knees and remain in contact with his knees for a period of 15 seconds by slightly touching them. The movement over the thighs should absorb one minute. Thus the whole pass should take a duration of 3 minutes. It would be absolutely necessary in the beginning to give some ten or twelve passes. During the process, suggestions should on no consideration be used.

After a short time ascertain the nature of sleep of your subject, whether deep or not, by the expression of his face and body. Do not make use of any other means to test his sleep. If you do so, you will spoil the future progress in clairvoyance. If you are sure that he is fast asleep and he is not able to open his eyes or hear you at your first call—"Mr. do you hear me;" make some more calls and he will respond. You can then proceed with the following instructions.

Sit by his side; hold your left hand fingers to his forehead at a distance of an inch and ask in a low positive tone, "Mr. do you hear me. Now I want you to see how many fingers I just hold above your head. Do you see it?" If he answers in the negative, make some quick passes "at distance" from the forehead to his chin, with your right hand and say very positively, "now you can plainly see my fingers; tell me the number." If he is still unable to plainly see your fingers, insist that he can see and suggest that nothing will obstruct his sight, etc. If all your efforts prove futile, request him to suggest any method whereby you can

make him see plainly, as the methods vary in persons
of different nature as to their characteristics. In 9
cases out of 10 your subject at that state will give you
a sure method. Generally, in almost all cases, what
we give will produce miracles and crown you with success. This test may be successful on the first day or it
may take you some days. Never be in a hurry or never
force results in him, give him his own time to succeed.
When you are successful with this test, proceed to multiply this at your discretion by various others, such as:
Holding pencils over his forehead and asking him to
give their correct number; applying a watch to the forehead and asking him to give you the correct time;
writing some letters on a card and holding it over his
head and thereby asking him to read them correctly;
and putting such cards in an envelope and then asking
him to read it, etc.

If you have a thorough satisfaction in the genuine-
ness of his answers, ask him to give you a good and
clear description of any place or places he has visited
in your neighborhood. If it is clear and precise, ask
him to describe any place or scene not far off your
place you have visited and which he has not. If you
are successful with this test then your complete success
in this branch of science is assured.

After this it would be better if you ask your
subject to read written words and thereon lead him
to sentences, verses and poems, etc. This should be
done before you enhance the distances of the places you
wish him to describe. You will be easily encouraged
by your subject to increase the distances of places, of
which he will gladly give you vivid and accurate descriptions. In this stage do not be misled but go on insist-
ing him to read the words, etc., referred to above.
When he correctly reads manuscripts, printed matter,
etc., at close quarters go on increasing the distance.
Simultaneously you may ask him to give you the descriptions of the places also.

You should take great care in asking him to read

anything which may not be lawfully brought to light; such should not be enforced upon the subject as such a proceedure is against an established code of moral principles of the spiritual realm, to which your subject becomes a denizen during the trances. Any violation of this will lead to terrible consequences. This *can in no way be misused*.

In the early stages of clairvoyance in your subject, your subject's language in the trance will be somewhat wanting and peculiar, when compared with his normal possibilities, since his mental vision will be imperfect then. Further you should understand not to force results or try to develop this psychic faculty in him in a week or two. You must not expect too much at once, for you will find that it requires considerable effort and persistency on your part to accomplish striking results. Due time should be allowed to your subject to attain a perfect state of psychic perception.

It is only by repeated trials, you will be able to bring your subject into trance. Do not be discouraged if you fail in the beginning. If you do not succeed within the first 10 or 15 trials, safely send the subject away and try some one else. It is very difficult to get proper subjects. You may have to try different persons till you pitch upon a proper one. Some may prove successful even in the first trial. Persevere and you will be crowned with success. When you conduct the trials, it would be better if you can so regulate the time as to hold the trials at one and the same time every day.

If by unavoidable or unforeseen circumstances any noise occurs your subject will turn into a sort of trance in which his behaviour may be either bordering on insanity or a thorough and splendid opening of the *unknown*. In either case do not be alarmed, but request him to come to the normal state and excuse you for any fault done consciously or unconsciously, and a spontaneous awakening will occur. Under any circumstances if he asks for time, do not allow him more than an hour at the most.

When you have fully developed your subject, you may not require so much time to bring him to the trance as in the early stages and you may even dispense with the passes. A mere word, sign, look or command or a very simple thought will throw the subject into trance. Do not try to accomplish this in a year or two.

CLAIRAUDIENCE.

As you continue your practice along this line, your subject will acquire the power of clairaudience (*i. e.*) the ability to hear and report you the conversation or any such of people at any distance, which is beyond the range of physical hearing. When this, however, is attained your subject can with no difficulty report to you the conversation of any who may speak, discuss or lecture at any distance.

RE-INCARNATION OR RE-BIRTH.

By the aid of mesmeric passes you can put the subject into a lucid stage in which he will be able to go back to his previous birth or births and give you vivid and clear accounts of those ages, etc.

In making the subject go back, great care should be taken and he should be asked to go stage by stage or year by year until the very womb, and then alone to the previous birth, and before awakenning him you should go over the same way to bring him back to the present circumstances. If he refuses, do not be discouraged; but patiently insist and he will positively come back.

Before undertaking the practice of Intent as well as Psychic Clairvoyances you will have to master the preparatory adjuncts—the proper conditions of bodily and mental relaxations and the fixing of your thoughts firmly, calmly and steadily upon any desired thing.

The mind should be brought under the control of the "will." Your "will" is now strong enough, but the mind requires being brought under the influence of the "will." When the mind is strengthened by will, it becomes a more powerful projector of thoughts and vibrations sent by the mind thus strengthened have much greater force and effect. As the body is to readily obey the commands of the mind, the control of the muscular movements should be thoroughly practiced. For which we append the following exercises:

EXERCISE I.

You should practice to *sit still* for 15 minutes together. This may seem to you to be a simple one, but when you try, you will find that it is an impossible feat. Lie down in a convenient posture either in an easy chair or in your bed and entirely relax all the muscles of your body and sit or lie still for 5 minutes. Gradually increase the time to 10 minutes and thence to 15 minutes.

EXERCISE II.

Take a sheet of stiff note paper and hold it by the thumb and two fingers at one corner and raise the arm to a level with the shoulder and hold it perfectly steady. Your gaze should be fixed on your arm. This should be practiced until you are able to hold it for 5 minutes. Both the arms should be well practiced. To see whether your hands are steady look at the tips of the fingers.

EXERCISE III.

Take a goblet full of water and hold it between the thumb and one finger and extend the arm in front of you. Gaze intently upon the glass, so that the least quivering may be noticed. This should be practiced until you are able to hold it for 5 minutes. These will aid you to control all involuntary muscular movements.

EXERCISE IV.

Raise your right arm to a level with the shoulder. Stiffen all the muscles of the arm from shoulder to hand by a simple act of the will. Do this six times. Do this with the left arm also; the right should then hang by the side lifeless.

EXERCISE V.

Close the thumb and fingers of the right hand and place the hand on the knee. The first finger must be pointed out in front of you (it need not be closed). Move this finger slowly from side to side. Your attention should be firmly implanted on the end of the finger.

EXERCISE VI.

Lie down with eyes closed on your back. Place your hands at your sides in contact with the body. Completely relax all the muscles of the body as in sleep. Inhale through the nostrils, slowly as much air as possible and keep them in the lungs for a few seconds—say 40 or 50—and slowly exhale every particle of air from the lungs through the mouth. Do this for 10 minutes. While exercising repeat mentally, "All my physical weakness, if any, is leaving me; I have no fatigue or uneasiness of body; I am all right." This will not only give you a great physical relief but also a great ease of mind.

These exercises may be *ad-infinitum* and we leave it to you, to supply them by your own ingenuity. What we have given is sufficient, as the principle idea being that the exercise shall consist of some trivial, familiar and monotonous muscular movement, and that attention *must* be firmly implanted on any moving part of the body.

EXERCISE VII.

To aid you in concentrating your thoughts upon a desired thing, some similar exercises as the following should be practiced until you conquer your rebellious spirit. This may seem to you to be a very simple thing and it is only when you try you will feel the difficulty of it. Nothing but insignificant and uninteresting articles should be taken, as you can easily hold your attention on interesting objects. For instance, take a piece of twine and concentrate your entire attention upon it for 5 minutes. Look at it intently; think of it; turn it over; consider it; think of its uses; its object; of the substance of which it is made; the place or places where it is made; the process of manufacture; the amount of energy required in manufacturing it, etc. Think of no other thing but the twine; you should think that the study of the history of that piece of twine is the sole aim of your life; you should think that nothing but that piece of twine and you exist in the world.

Now, after having performed the above exercises, you may safely enter into the realm of Clairvoyance.

INTENT CLAIRVOYANCE.

The method we give you below, is the most successful one invented by the greatest of our forefathers and specially handed to us by a renowned soul to develop artificially the faculty of clairvoyance in man. This compares very favourably with the ordinary crystal gazing method and is in every way superior to it. We speak of practical experience and have had undeniable evidence of clairvoyance presented through this means. If you follow our instructions and do just as we tell you, you will become a successful clairvoyant in an incredibly short time.

HOW TO CULTIVATE CLAIRVOYANCE

Get a small quantity of printing ink—say five drops,

—mix it well with two drops of turpentine; then put the paste on a glass piece or on a green leaf (maple leaf preferred), make a circle having a diameter of one-eighth of an inch. Retire into a quiet dark room; light a single lamp; keep it on a raised level on the northern side of your seat, so that the reflection may come from the north. Keep the leaf with the circle of paste in its middle in your left palm and hold it within a distance of one to two feet from the lamp, so that a distinct ray of light may fall on the paste. Then attain a state of passivity by relaxing your mind and body and look intently, without winking, in the reflection created on the paste. After a short time, small luminous circles will appear and gradually develop into bigger ones; some shape or figure will burst in. If you continue to look at it, these forms will take a definite course. By continuous practice, past and present events will be clearly depicted and enacted before you. When you attain this state at will, command any scene or scenes which might have occurred or occur in future, wherein you might not have been aware of or unable to know the perpetrators or parties concerned, and thus find out the actors. By the aid of this, hidden treasure, lost property, murders, crimes, robberies, etc., can be easily brought home to the guilty parties.

PSYCHIC CLAIRVOYANCE.

What Yoga or Psychic Clairvoyance depicts we have in the learned words of Col. H. S. Olcott: "Among the Siddhis (spiritual power) which develop themselves in the course of the Indian system of psychic training called Yoga, is one which gives the ascetic knowledge of the 'seven worlds' or 'seven places' of evolution. All veils before nature, all masks that hide her face from man are torn away, the hidden becomes exposed, the clouds of ignorance dissolve, the sun of knowledge shines, the yogee hears the latent as well as the non-vibrating sounds, reads the pages of the past, present and future with equal ease, sees whatever he fixes his thoughts upon, whether happening this moment or at a period milleniums back."

From the above you can understand what immense benefits and what eternal soul bliss awaits a Yogi or rather the practitioner of Psychic Clairvoyance.

We give you here the surest and best method to develop Yoga or Psychic Clairvoyance. Follow the instructions implicitly and you are sure to succeed. No time can be fixed for this, as the time to obtain your goal in this varies as to your characteristics and temperaments. Some do succeed within an incredibly short time of 2 or 3 months and with some it takes 2 or 3 years. Work patiently and at last as sure as the sun shines you will one day succeed. Your toil will not go in vain.

HOW TO DEVELOP CLAIRVOYANCE.

Go into a perfectly dark room and sit down on an easy chair letting your feet rest squarely upon the floor.

A very good instrument to use to assist one in development is what is known as the *Lunar Circle*, which is covered with a secret preparation so that it can be seen in the darkest room. A Lunar Circle can be obtained from *The de Laurence Company. See Order No. 231* in their great book Catalogue.

The *Lunar Circle* should be hung on the wall about four or five feet from your chair and so it is on a level with your eyes. Then place your left thumb in the hollow of your right palm; close the fingers of your right hand over it. Rest your hands thus joined over the pit of your stomach. Relax your mind and body. Remain passive; gazing steadily at the *Lunar Circle* without winking. Now commence the deep breathing process explained to you under "WILL POWER DEVELOPMENT" for a period of thirty minutes. You will not at first be able to do this for thirty minutes but you will have to practice and lengthen the time by degrees. After practicing the above exercise, for a short time you should perceive a light blue white aura near the outside of the *Lunar Circle*. As you continue to practice the light may become stronger and increase in lustre and area. At times the room may become illuminated by a strong Astral Light so that things in the room about you may become visible. Again, you may observe a column of blue etheric waves passing before your eyes. Indeed there may appear several light waves of bright colors of the aura, such as *blue*, *yellow*, and *red*. Further, you may see a blue sparkling star like light in glittering circles. These are manifestations of spirit or Astral lights which usually surround one when in the elementary stage of Clairvoyance. The blue sparkling starlike light, referred to above, may change into a white sparkling manifestation.

These spirit or Astral lights are likely to appear in any part of the room and if your practicing is continued it is very likely that spirit faces will begin to materialise to you. It may be added, however, that many claim to get better and quicker results if a little Temple Incense is burned or some Waxen Candles are used for a few minutes during the exercise. Mental requests should be thrown out and made for more spirit light and better materialization. Spirit faces appear only gradually at first, but in time they should become quite clear.

Under such circumstances continue your daily practice with all earnestness and determination for further improvement, and you will see the perfect form of a human spiritual being. You may speak to him mentally to develop further, and very probably you may notice nodding of its head or a motion of its hands recognising your mental suggestions. At this stage request earnestly that spiritual being to give you more light and at once all necessary help will flow to you.

After you get a clear view of them, make them move in different directions by means of "will commands." Some may and some may not respond to your commands. After a little acquaintance with them you will see your wishes are acted up to.

When you have developed this stage, you may request the spirits to move any furniture from one place to another and do some service to you. And in course of time you may request them for information on any subject. Before the perfect development or even before the very clear appearance of the faces or spirit, you may notice a noise as the report of a small pistol. If you hear such a noise, do not be afraid; such noises are habitual before the appearance. If the noise becomes more audible your clairaudient power will be developed unconsciously and after a time you will be able through the aid of the higher ways to hear whatever you want.

Dear Reader! This is no toy to be played with. Even now you may not understand the grave significance of your more or less superhuman power. For Heaven's sake do not misuse the power. Do not compel the spirit to disclose any fact or facts that are not intended for your ears. Never cause the movement of things by the spiritual agency to satisfy the whim and fancy of any, even though he or she is as dear to you as your life. When your conversation with the spirit improves and progresses, you will know who you are.

THE END OF BOOK THREE.

FINIS.

LaVergne, TN USA
09 December 2010

208064LV00005B/48/P